European Heritage, Dialogue and Digital Practices

European Heritage, Dialogue and Digital Practices focuses on the intersection of heritage, dialogue and digital culture in the context of Europe. Responding to the increased emphasis on the potential for heritage and digital technologies to foster dialogue and engender communitarian identities in Europe, the book explores what kind of role digital tools, platforms and practices play in supporting and challenging dialogue about heritage in the region.

Drawing on fieldwork involving several European museums and heritage organisations, the chapters in this volume critically engage with the role of digital technology in heritage work and its association with ideas of democratisation, multivocality and possibilities for feedback and dialogic engagement in the emerging digital public sphere. The book also provides a framework for understanding dialogue in relation to other commonly used approaches in heritage institutions, such as participation, engagement and intercultural exchange. The authors map out the complex landscape of digitally mediated heritage practices in Europe, both official and unofficial, by capturing three distinct areas of practice: perceptions and applications of digitally mediated dialogues around heritage within European museums and cultural policy, facilitation of dialogue between European museums and communities through participatory design approaches and non-official mobilisation of heritage on social media.

European Heritage, Dialogue and Digital Practices will be of interest to both scholars and students in the fields of heritage and museum studies, digital heritage, media studies and communication, the digital humanities, sociology and memory studies. The book will also appeal to policy makers and professionals working in a variety of fields.

Areti Galani is a Senior Lecturer in Media, Culture, Heritage at Newcastle University, UK, specialising in digital cultural heritage. She works with people-centred methodologies and research-through-design approaches to explore the role of digital technologies in heritage contexts, on-site and online. She has published on issues related to empathy, reflexivity and sociality in designing and evaluating [digitally mediated] heritage experiences.

Rhiannon Mason is a Professor of Heritage and Cultural Studies and the head of the School of Arts and Cultures in Newcastle University, UK. Her research and teaching are focused on heritage, identity and nationalism, and she has published extensively around these topics as well as issues of emotion, memory and migration.

Gabi Arrigoni is a Researcher at Newcastle University, UK, in the field of digital cultural heritage. She focuses on future and design-based methods for heritage scholarship.

Critical Heritages of Europe
Series editors: Christopher Whitehead and Susannah Eckersley, both at the University of Newcastle, UK

The *Critical Heritages of Europe* series seeks to explore the cultural and social politics of the European past in the present. Bridging theoretical and empirical research, the series accommodates broad understandings of Europe – a shifting and historically mutable entity, made both of internal tensions and exogenous encounters, re-imaginings and influences. 'Heritage' too is taken as an expansive paradigm, made in myriad practices where the past is valorised for the present, from folk traditions to museums and memorials, the management of historic sites and traditions, and everyday matters such as education, political discourse, home life, food consumption and people's relations with place.

Books in the series engage with European heritages in *critical* times – in all senses – when Europe and mobilizations of its heritages and memories are called upon to solve problems, and when contests over the meanings of the past are part of wider social and political relations and tensions. Heritage practices are variously informed by civil and uncivil visions, the politics of difference and co-presence, difficult pasts, relations with the 'outside', borders, margins, and migrations. Critical questions include:

- What is the European past made to do in the present and for the future?
- What counts as European heritage? To whom, and why?
- How and why do relationships with, and attitudes to, the past inform identity positions, social orders and moral values in, or in relation to, Europe?
- When and where in the (wider) world do European heritages configure identities?
- What are the contemporary meanings and effects of global encounters, mobilities and trajectories in which Europe has played roles?
- What theoretical and critical perspectives can be articulated to contribute new understandings of European heritages? How might these be made relevant for current and future heritage practice?

- What are the relations between theory, criticality, ethics and heritage practice in the European dimension?

Classical Heritage and European Identities
The Imagined Geographies of Danish Classicism
Lærke Maria Andersen Funder, Troels Myrup Kristensen and Vinnie Nørskov

Heritage and Festivals in Europe
Performing Identities
Edited by Ullrich Kockel, Cristina Clopot, Baiba Tjarve and Máiréad Nic Craith

Dimensions of Heritage and Memory
Multiple Europes and the Politics of Crisis
Edited by Christopher Whitehead, Susannah Eckersley, Gönül Bozoğlu, and Mads Daugbjerg

European Heritage, Dialogue and Digital Practices
Edited by Areti Galani, Rhiannon Mason and Gabi Arrigoni

European Memory in Populism
Representations of Self and Other
Edited by Chiara De Cesari and Ayhan Kaya

For more information about this series, please visit: www.routledge.com/Critical-Heritages-of-Europe/book-series/COHERE

European Heritage, Dialogue and Digital Practices

Edited by Areti Galani, Rhiannon Mason and Gabi Arrigoni

LONDON AND NEW YORK

First published 2020 by Routledge

2 Park Square, Milton Park, Abingdon, Oxon, OX14 4RN
605 Third Avenue, New York, NY 10017

Routledge is an imprint of the Taylor & Francis Group, an informa business

First issued in paperback 2020

Copyright © 2020 selection and editorial matter, Areti Galani, Rhiannon Mason and Gabi Arrigoni; individual chapters, the contributors

The right of Areti Galani, Rhiannon Mason and Gabi Arrigoni to be identified as the authors of the editorial material, and of the authors for their individual chapters, has been asserted in accordance with sections 77 and 78 of the Copyright, Designs and Patents Act 1988.

All rights reserved. No part of this book may be reprinted or reproduced or utilised in any form or by any electronic, mechanical, or other means, now known or hereafter invented, including photocopying and recording, or in any information storage or retrieval system, without permission in writing from the publishers.

Notice:
Product or corporate names may be trademarks or registered trademarks, and are used only for identification and explanation without intent to infringe.

The Open Access version of this book, available at www.taylorfrancis.com, has been made available under a Creative Commons Attribution-Non Commercial-No Derivatives 4.0 license.

British Library Cataloguing-in-Publication Data
A catalogue record for this book is available from the British Library

Library of Congress Cataloging-in-Publication Data
A catalog record for this book has been requested

ISBN: 978-0-367-14806-5 (hbk)
ISBN: 978-0-367-78788-2 (pbk)

Typeset in Times New Roman
by Apex CoVantage, LLC

To our transnational families

Contents

List of figures xi
List of contributors xii
Acknowledgements xiv

1 Introduction: locating heritage and dialogue in
   digital culture 1
   ARETI GALANI, GABI ARRIGONI, RHIANNON MASON AND
   BETHANY REX

2 Problematising digital and dialogic heritage practices
   in Europe: tensions and opportunities 9
   ARETI GALANI, KATIE MARKHAM AND RHIANNON MASON

3 Digitally enhanced polyvocality and reflective spaces:
   challenges in sustaining dialogue in museums through
   digital technologies 37
   GABI ARRIGONI AND ARETI GALANI

   Artefact vignette #1: *Transformation Machine* 60
   ANNELIE BERNER, MONIKA HALINA SEYFRIED, GABI ARRIGONI
   AND ARETI GALANI

4 Participation and dialogue: curatorial reflexivity in
   participatory processes 62
   DAGNY STUEDAHL, TORHILD SKÅTUN, AGELIKI LEFKADITOU AND
   TOBIAS MESSENBRINK

Contents

Artefact vignette #2: *The New Europe* app   84
ANNELIE BERNER, MONIKA HALINA SEYFRIED, GABI ARRIGONI AND ARETI GALANI

5 **1215 in 280 characters: talking about *Magna Carta* on Twitter**   86
DAVID FARRELL-BANKS

Artefact vignette #3: *Erdi*   107
ANNELIE BERNER, MONIKA HALINA SEYFRIED, GABI ARRIGONI AND ARETI GALANI

6 **Dialogues and heritages in the digital public sphere**   109
ARETI GALANI, RHIANNON MASON AND BETHANY REX

Index   122

Figures

3.1 *Memory and Migration*, contemporary section, at Galata Museo del Mare   45
3.2 *The Diversity Triangle* at Museum for Intercultural Dialogue   49
3.3 *The emancipation of the Jews – historical debates 1801–1912* at the Jewish Museum Berlin   50
4.1 The digital installation *The sound of FOLK*   65
4.2 The participatory process of *The Sound of FOLK* lasted over eight workshops   72
4.3 Future Workshop, the phantasy phase   74
5.1 A conversation between two individuals in the 'reply' thread to Tweet 4   98
5.2 The Magna Carta Memorial at Runneymede, erected by the American Bar Association   100

Contributors

Annelie Berner is an Interaction Designer and Researcher. She works across disciplines, from ethics to data technologies. She is a faculty member and researcher at CIID (Copenhagen Institute of Interaction Design), where she teaches programming and data visualisation.

David Farrell-Banks is a Doctoral Researcher in Media, Culture, Heritage at Newcastle University, UK, whose work focuses upon uses of the past in political discourse.

Ageliki Lefkaditou is Senior Curator at the Norwegian Museum of Science and Technology. Her work focuses on contemporary and historical understandings of biopolitical practices and materialities, museum theory and practice. She has curated the exhibition *FOLK – From racial types to DNA sequences* and has published on transnational human diversity research.

Katie Markham is a Researcher at Newcastle University UK, where she specialises in the study of empathy as it relates to post-conflict heritage and tourism.

Tobias Messenbrink has recently submitted his master's thesis to the Department of Informatics, University of Oslo. He started his career as a sound technician, later moving into web design and digital design as well as working as a museum technician. He currently works as an IT Consultant in Oslo.

Bethany Rex is a Research Fellow in the Innovation Insights Hub, University of the Arts London. Her main interest is in the effects of austerity on local museum services and meaning systems in arts and cultural organisations.

Monika Halina Seyfried is an Interaction Designer with a background in art, photography and filmmaking and expertise in immersive experiences.

Her work has been exhibited in several cities across the globe, including Beijing, Paris, Copenhagen and Zagreb.

Torhild Skåtun works as Educator and Developer of learning activities at the Norwegian Museum of Science and Technology. She is currently on the PhD programme in museums studies at Leicester.

Dagny Stuedahl is Professor at the Department of Journalism and Media Studies, Oslo Metropolitan University. Along with her academic career, she has a dual and interdisciplinary focus on humanities, social sciences and an applied approaches to design of digital media, relating these to research fields as media literacy, science and technology studies (STS), participatory design, co-design and the emerging field digital cultural Heritage.

Acknowledgements

We would like to thank the cultural institutions and organisations and all individual members of staff who contributed to this volume as interviewees or through hosting activities and facilitating our visits to their institutions. The research that underpins all contributions to this volume would have not be possible without their generosity. We also extend our gratitude to all research participants, co-creators, co-designers, friends and members of the public who, through their participation in our activities, workshops and public events, allowed us to gain insights into their practices around heritage, dialogue and digital technologies and shaped our understandings of the issues examined by this volume.

We thank all the authors of this volume for their thought-provoking contributions, their commitment to a tight schedule and the attention and patience with which they engaged with the reviewing and editorial process. We also extend our thanks to the Routledge editorial board for supporting this project as well the anonymous reviewers of the original book proposal, who helped us to focus our ideas and tighten the structure of the volume.

We also acknowledge that this book was possible only as part of the larger CoHERE research project and collaborative effort undertaken by all the project partners and researchers. In particular, we acknowledge the contribution of the project leaders and our colleagues, Professor Chris Whitehead and Dr Susannah Eckersley, who guided us through the development of the book proposal and the editorial process. Our collaborations and discussions with our partners in Work Package 4 have informed our thinking and inspired the contents of this volume. CoHERE has received funding from the European Union Horizon 2020 programme under grant agreement NO 693289.

The ideas expressed in this volume started occupying our conversations almost five years ago, when Rhiannon and Areti were awarded two small grants from Newcastle University's Institute for Social Renewal (NISR) and Institute for Creative Arts Practice (NICAP), respectively, to carry out research on how ideas of identity, place and belonging and digital creative practice can be fruitfully explored in relation to the notion of 'the dialogic museum'. We are grateful to NISR and NICAP for supporting our early methodological and design experimentations on the topic as well as all our generous colleagues, partners and participants in those mini-projects. Ideas, experiences and connections developed in those projects enabled us to think through some of the dilemmas and realities faced by heritage practitioners and individuals in relation to dialogue and inspired the emphasis on practice that characterises this volume.

Our own writings in this volume have also benefited from the generosity of our colleagues in Newcastle University, who encouraged us throughout the process and were able to provide us with relief of other tasks at times of pressure. We would especially like to thank Dr Joanne Sayner for always finding the time to read drafts so thoughtfully and encouragingly, no matter how busy she was. We are indebted to Dr Kostas Arvanitis (University of Manchester) for many inspiring discussions about digital cultural heritage, dialogue and the [digital] public sphere over the years.

Last, but by no means least, we thank our young families, Richard and Ellie, Alistair and Alexander, Tom, Olli and Vali, for asking us regularly 'how our story is going' and telling us with conviction and enthusiasm, 'you can do it mummy!' Without their support and patience this volume would have not materialised. Ellie, Alexander, Olli and Vali – we did it!

1 Introduction

Locating heritage and dialogue in digital culture

Areti Galani, Gabi Arrigoni, Rhiannon Mason and Bethany Rex

In 2010, Intercult founder Chris Torch, reflecting on the position and role of European museums in a globalised world, and specifically in relation to digital technologies and platforms, made the following points:

> The raw material of mutual understanding is accessible in ways never before imagined. But this capacity for increased distribution is not enough to generate true intercultural dialogue. It is the cross-fertilisation between virtual access and face to face encounter which makes museums relevant and useful.
>
> (Torch, 2010)

Since then, significant developments have taken place on the technological, cultural and political front, and a number of European policies and initiatives have focused on the role of intercultural dialogue in Europe (Council of Europe, 2008; European Commission, 2018). Despite the institutional recognition of the role of culture and heritage as tools for dialogue between nations (Anderson, O'Dowd and Wilson, 2003; Innocenti, 2016) and the significant investment in the digitisation of European cultural resources (European Commission, 2012; Valtysson, 2012), work that examines how the areas of European heritage, dialogue and digital culture intersect remains less common.

This *Focus* volume aims to provide a synergistic exploration of the three areas of heritage, dialogue and digital (to include technologies and practices) to highlight two things: (a) the plurality of understandings, terms and definitions of European heritage, dialogue and digital within European heritage institutions; and (b) the discrepancies and tensions that arise in both the conceptualisation and articulation of their interrelationships.

With regard to the former, the volume contributes to the discourse on the 'dialogic museum' by critically reflecting on the lack of common language and understandings in both conceptualising and practically mobilising dialogue in heritage institutions. It builds on existing research which has already identified a significant diversity in the language around dialogue used by European cultural institutions (Bodo, 2013). Regarding the latter, the volume revisits and problematises some of the commonly circulating assumptions, such as the role of intercultural dialogue relating to heritage to support positive outcomes and the creation of harmonious societies and the inherent capacity of digital technologies to democratise heritage and to create transcultural dialogues. Therefore, it makes clearer the increasing need for other-than-instrumental uses of dialogue, heritage and digital in the context of European identity building.

Furthermore, this *Focus* volume discusses original empirical research that specifically focuses on the intersection between European heritage, dialogic and digital practices. This empirical research has been carried out within European cultural institutions and among online communities that engage with what Leggewie (2010) calls the 'seven circles of European memory', such as colonialism, the memory of the First and Second World Wars, the trauma of the Holocaust, transnational immigration and the flagship values of democracy, peace and integration that underpin Europe's narrative post 1945 (online). Drawing on this research, the volume considers the emergence and role of digitally mediated dialogues around heritage in Europe within two continua: (a) dialogues taking place between institutions and individuals and (b) official and unofficial narratives. The scale and diversity of voices taking part in these dialogues is also explored.

It is not our intention to claim that the topics of European heritage, dialogue and digital technologies and culture have not received scholarly attention; quite the opposite. The individual topics and the individual intersections of these areas of activity have been researched for some time. For instance, the discourse around heritage and digital technologies has been active since the 1990s (Jones-Garmil, 1997; Mintz and Thomas, 1998; Parry, 2007; Cameron and Kenderdine, 2007, among others). This discourse adopted existing frameworks such as Malraux's 'museum without walls' as well as generated new ones, such as the 'networked' (Proctor, 2008) and, more recently, the 'connected museum' (Drotner and Schrøder, 2013) to vividly describe the new and emerging nature of cultural institutions in digital culture. In these conceptualisations, the notion of dialogue is both implicitly and explicitly explored, and digital platforms and tools are identified as having the capacity to open opportunities for institutions to have a dialogic relationship with existing and new audiences, within and beyond their physical boundaries.

Indeed, networked communication practices have had a profound impact on cultural as well as civic behaviours, affecting the scale and quality of exchange between individuals, as well as between individuals and organisations across geographical and, as media theorists argue, cultural boundaries:

Introduction 3

Global turmoil prompts citizens to learn more about each other, and digital media fuel intercultural communication on a scale and of a kind that is a significant departure from the mass-mediated contacts of the last several centuries.

(Smith Pfister and Soliz, 2011, p. 246)

The contributions to this volume specifically focus on the question whether the dialogic potential of digital technologies, outlined by media theorists and digital heritage researchers, is also materialised (or not) in heritage practice and how European policy encourages (or not) a dialogic focus within digital heritage work. Do specific institutional and policy conditions as well as different conceptualisations of dialogue and digital technologies among heritage professionals and stakeholders enable or encumber the dialogic potential of digital technologies in the context of European heritage?

The connection between heritage institutions and dialogue has also received significant attention since the 1980s alongside the advancement of theories such as 'new museology' (Vergo, 1989), which argued for a greater connection between cultural institutions and their audiences. An influential text in this discourse is John Kuo Wei Tchen's (1992) account of the *Chinatown History Museum Experiment* in New York, which sought to engage with communities connected to New York's Chinatown to 'mutually explor[e] the memory and meaning of Chinatown's past' in order to improve 'the planning and development of the organisation' (p. 291). Furthermore, the idea of dialogue has received renewed attention in institutional heritage practice in connection to the notion of the 'participatory museum' (e.g. Simon, 2010; Adair, Filene and Koloski, 2011). However, Tchen's writing is particularly relevant to the preoccupation of this volume with the relationship between dialogue and alterity, because it specifically alerts us to the fact that any dialogue between institutions and communities should necessarily recognise that communities themselves are multicultural, internally diverse and fluid, emerging through continuous interactions between people and places.

In the European context, the relationship between cultural institutions and their communities has also been pursued under the auspices of intercultural dialogue, and the policies, research and practice associated with it. Intercultural dialogue presumes that museums and cultural institutions become 'space[s] for negotiation' that should also 'question the social segmentation resulting from multicultural policies, in which the recognition of cultural diversity and distinct identities often ends up reinforcing discrimination and segregation' (Delgado, 2009, p. 8). Furthermore, Harrison (2013) urges us to consider heritage as inherently 'dialogical' as a means to acknowledging that all heritage emerges through negotiation between human and non-human actors and, as such, it should aim to engage with contemporary economic, environmental, political and social concerns too. One might argue that such texts aim to encourage us to think purposively and analytically about heritage institutions and their possibilities. This proposition seems particularly important given the current political and social context within which heritage institutions in Europe are operating. However, the future-oriented, transformative tone of these ideas make a challenging reading as they propose dialogue and digital as drivers that enable heritage practice to attend to slogans such as 'valuing diversity' (UK government), 'unity in diversity' (European Commission) and 'we transform the world with culture!' (*Europeana*) and their accompanying policy statements. This is more so in the light of recent retreats away from internationalism made most visible by the recent Brexit vote in the UK (in 2016) and the rise of right-wing and populist politics across Europe and across the Atlantic. Addressing propositions for a digitally mediated 'dialogic heritage' in such contexts where alterity is not readily considered in a celebratory mode exposes the real-world stakes in this discussion. At stake here is the possibility for heritage institutions to not only *commit to*, but regarding the case-study institutions which this volume examines, to *design for* dialogic practice within their actual spaces and alongside existing digital platforms, such as social media sharing platforms and Twitter. This volume, therefore, asks the question of what the possibilities for dialogue and dialogic heritage practice might be, both in the European context and in relation to established and emerging digital practices in an expanding and diverse digital public sphere.

Building on the significant corpus of research briefly outlined earlier, this *Focus* volume is intended as a particular 'snapshot' in time, which allows us to discuss and reflect upon the practices that take place in the intersections of heritage, dialogue and digital transformations in the context of Europe. It is not intended as a comprehensive exploration of the terms 'European heritage', 'digital technologies', 'digital culture' and 'dialogue' and all their ramifications. In this respect, we recognise and fully acknowledge that these are not only vast topics in their own right but they are also non-fixed entities; rather, to borrow from José van Dijck (2012, p. 5), they evolve alongside the social practices that compose them.

The volume, therefore, articulates a particular interest in digitally mediated dialogic heritage *practices*, that is, how ideas, beliefs or methods about heritage, dialogue and digital are brought together through their application and mobilisation in the context of European heritage institutions and their publics. By putting an emphasis on practice, we wish to acknowledge its capacity to illustrate, embody and contradict both theoretical ideas and policy imperatives in the nexus of European heritage, dialogue and digital culture. We are inspired in this decision by Keller's (2011) observation that 'a theory of life as dialogic can lead us to ignore the actual experience of an everyday life that frequently seems obsessively bound instead to the monologic' (p. 30). We also align with a prevalent recent emphasis among heritage scholars on the significance of attending to practice in approaching topics such as heritage narratives (Smith, 2011), memory and heritage in Europe (Macdonald, 2013) and affect in relation to heritage (Wetherell, 2012). To summarise using Reckwitz's (2002) words: 'a practice is thus a routinised way in which bodies are moved, objects are handled, subjects are treated, things are described and the world is understood' (p. 250). In this respect, all practices are by nature social practices. This also applies to digital practices, which Jones, Chik and Hafner (2015) describe as '"assemblages" of actions involving tools associated with digital technologies, which have come to be recognised by specific groups of people as ways of attaining particular social goals, enacting particular social identities, and reproducing particular sets of social relationships' (p. 3). The emphasis on museum practices is present in this volume through Chapters 3, 4 and 5 as well as through the three 'artefact vignettes' that further provide insights into design practices in this context.

In Chapter 2 of this volume Galani, Markham and Mason revisit individual European policies on cultural heritage, intercultural dialogue and digital technologies for heritage to identify points of conversion and diversion on how dialogue is understood and to reflect on key tensions arising from these policies, such as the role of intercultural dialogue and access to heritage resources to support harmonious societies in the context of digital public sphere. Subsequently, the volume presents three *loci* in which digitally mediated dialogues around heritage are explored in relation to museological and heritage practices. Arrigoni and Galani (Chapter 3) draw on interviews with museum professionals and display analysis in ten European museums to discuss how *institutions* approach the role of digital technologies to support dialogue as part of their institutional philosophy and how this is manifested in their exhibition spaces. Stuedahl *et al.* (Chapter 4) reflect on digital co-creation practices between curators in the Norwegian Museum of Science and Technology in Oslo and a *group of multicultural youth* to discuss the dialogic affordances of creating a public-facing digital participatory exhibit; Farrell-Banks (Chapter 5) explores the nature of Twitter as a platform for digitally mediated dialogues around European heritage by examining the use of *Magna Carta* by right-wing populist groups and their online local/global audiences alongside the mobilisation of the same heritage by heritage institutions in the UK.

Each of these chapters is followed by an 'artefact vignette' that introduces a speculative digital artefact which addresses the key themes of the chapter.

These artefacts were created as part of the EU-funded CoHERE project using a research-through-design approach and were deployed in festival, workshop and living lab contexts in European cities in 2017–2018. The three vignettes aim to introduce a dialogic element in the overall structure of the volume. All three vignettes together are also proposed as a mini-portfolio, a triptych, of design experimentation to advocate the role of critical, playful digital design in the context of heritage and dialogic practices *at large*, a topic we come back to in the concluding chapter of this volume.

The volume concludes with a chapter by Galani, Mason and Rex (Chapter 6) that reflects on the critical issues and the juxtapositions emerging from the three *loci* of practice explored in Chapters 3, 4 and 5. It observes that two epistemological approaches emerge through the analysis: *dialogue-as-purpose* and *dialogue-as-purposive*. It further proposes that heritage organisations in the networked digital public sphere are well suited to engage with *dialogue as reflexive action* and *dialogue as purposeful listening*. While acknowledging and elaborating on the limitations of dialogue, the concluding chapter also articulates ways forward for digitally mediated dialogic practices in European heritage, through *the adoption of design methods*, the development of *hybrid, techno-social literacies* and the *linking up of relevant policies and strategies* that underpin the tripartite relationship between European heritage, dialogue and digital culture.

Acknowledgements

This research was carried out as part of the project CoHERE (2016–2019), which has received funding from the European Union Horizon 2020 programme under grant agreement NO 693289.

References

Adair, B., Filene, B. and Koloski, L. (2011) *Letting go? Sharing historical authority in a user-generated world*. Philadelphia: The Pew Centre for Arts & Heritage.

Anderson, J., O'Dowd, L. and Wilson, T. M. (2003) 'Culture, co-operation and borders', in *Culture and Cooperation in Europe's Borderland*. Amsterdam and New York: Brill Rodopi, pp. 13–29.

Bodo, S. (2013) 'New paradigms for intercultural work in museums – Or intercultural work as a new paradigm for museum practice?', in Sīmansone, I. Z. (ed.), *Museums and intercultural dialogue the learning museum network project report NR 4*. Regione Emilia-Romagna: The Learning Museum Network.

Cameron, F. and Kenderdine, S. (eds.) (2007) *Theorizing digital cultural heritage: A critical discourse*. Cambridge, MA: MIT Press.

Council of Europe. (2008) *White paper on intercultural dialogue: "Living together as equals in dignity"*. Strasbourg: Council of Europe Publishing.

Delgado, E. (2009) 'Museums as spaces of negotiation', in Bodo, S., Gibbs, K. and Sani, M. (eds.), *Museums as places for intercultural dialogue: Selected practices from Europe*. Regione Emilia-Romagna: Map for ID Group, pp. 8–9.

Drotner, K. and Schrøder, K. (2013) *Museum communication and social media*. New York: Routledge.

European Commission. (2012) *Digitising our cultural heritage*. Available at: https://ec.europa.eu/digital-single-market/en/news/digitising-our-cultural-heritage (Accessed: 13 January 2018).

European Commission. (2018) *Intercultural dialogue*. Available at: https://ec.europa.eu/culture/policy/strategic-framework/intercultural-dialogue_en (Accessed: 13 January 2018).

Harrison, R. (2013) *Heritage: Critical approaches*. London and New York: Routledge.

Innocenti, P. (2016) *Migrating heritage: Experiences of cultural networks and cultural dialogue in Europe*. London and New York: Routledge.

Jones, R. H., Chik, A. and Hafner, C. A. (2015) *Discourse and digital practices*. London and New York: Routledge.

Jones-Garmil, K. (ed.) (1997) *The wired museum: Emerging technology and changing paradigms*. Washington, DC: American Association of Museums.

Keller, J. (2011) 'Dialogue as moral paradigm: Paths towards intercultural interaction', *Policy Futures in Education*, 9(1), pp. 29–34.

Leggewie, C. (2010) 'Seven circles of European memory', *Eurozine*. Available at: www.eurozine.com/seven-circles-of-european-memory (Accessed: 7 January 2019).

Macdonald, S. (2013) *Memorylands: Heritage and identity in Europe today*. London and New York: Routledge.

Mintz, A. P. and Thomas, S. (eds.) (1998) *The virtual and the real: Media in the museum*. Washington, DC: American Association of Museums.

Parry, R. (2007) *Recoding the museum: Digital heritage and the technologies of change*. London and New York: Routledge.

Proctor, N. (2008) 'Outside in the Agora: Mobile interpretation and Socratic dialogue in the networked museum', *Keynote presentation at the Dutch Digital Heritage Conference*, Rotterdam.

Reckwitz, A. (2002) 'Toward a theory of social practices: A development in culturalist theorizing', *European Journal of Social Theory*, 5(2), pp. 243–263.

Simon, N. (2010) *The participatory museum*. Santa Cruz: Museum 2.0.

Smith, L. (2011) 'The "doing" of heritage: Heritage as performance', in Jackson, A. and Kidd, J. (eds.), *Performing heritage research, practice and development in museum theatre and live interpretation*. Manchester: Manchester University Press, pp. 69–81.

Smith Pfister, D. and Soliz, J. (2011) '(Re)conceptualizing intercultural communication in a networked society', *Journal of International and Intercultural Communication*, 4(4), pp. 246–251.

Tchen, J. K. W. (1992) 'Creating a dialogic museum: The Chinatown history museum experiment', in Karp, I., Mullen Kreamer, C. and Levine, S. (eds.), *Museums and communities: The politics of public culture*. Washington, DC: Smithsonian Institution Press, pp. 285–326.

Torch, C. (2010) 'European museums and interculture, responding to challenges in a globalised world', *Stockholm*. Available at: http://panorama.intercultural-europe.org/_files/20110721-European%20Museums%20&%20Interculture-Torch%202011.pdf. (Accessed: 7 January 2019).

Valtysson, B. (2012) 'EUROPEANA: The digital construction of Europe's collective memory', *Information, Communication & Society*, 15(2), pp. 151–170.

Van Dijck, J. (2012) *The culture of connectivity*. Oxford: Oxford University Press.

Vergo, P. (1989) *The new museology*. London: Reaktion Books.

Wetherell, M. (2012) *Affect and emotion: A new social science understanding*. London: Sage Publications.

2 Problematising digital and dialogic heritage practices in Europe

Tensions and opportunities

Areti Galani, Katie Markham and Rhiannon Mason

Situating digital dialogues in the EU policy landscape

Within a European context, the position of dialogue as a means for addressing significant social conflict gained prominence just over a decade ago through two interlinked and currently active agendas, the *Faro Convention on the Value of Cultural Heritage for Society* (*Faro Convention* hereinafter) (Council of Europe, 2005) and the *White Paper on Intercultural Dialogue – Living Together As Equals in Dignity* (*White Paper on ICD* hereinafter) (Council of Europe, 2008). Both published by the Council of Europe, the former commits to 'promote dialogue among cultures and religions' by treating all cultural heritages 'equitably' (Council of Europe, 2005, preamble), whereas the latter proposes dialogue as a key to Europe's future and defines intercultural dialogue as

> an open and respectful exchange of views between individuals, groups with different ethnic, cultural, religious and linguistic backgrounds and heritage on the basis of mutual understanding and respect. It operates at all levels – within societies, between the societies of Europe and between Europe and the wider world.
>
> (Council of Europe, 2008, p. 10)

Both documents articulate dialogue as a means to achieving convergence around the European values of 'human rights, democracy and the rule of law' – both documents use the same phrase – by promoting knowledge around the different cultures as well as respect for diversity in both cultural expressions and interpretations, at the level of ethics and practices.

Remarkably, both of these influential programmatic documents make only limited mention of digital culture and practices: in the case of the *Faro Convention*, digital is evoked through the reference in Article 14 to the

Information Society with specific focus on enhancing 'access' to diverse heritages while protecting intellectual property rights; on the other hand, in the 61 pages of the *White Paper on ICD*, the word 'digital' appears once, with reference to digital broadcasting, while the phrase 'virtual spaces' makes a more productive appearance, only once in the document, in the section about 'spaces for intercultural dialogue' (Council of Europe, 2008, p. 32). Conversely, significant emphasis is placed on media, primarily in the form of media industries and their ability to render 'national cultural systems increasingly porous' (ibid., p. 13) and to act as 'critical spaces for indirect dialogue' (ibid., p. 33) by making visible cultural diversity to people who do not have first-hand experience of it. Notably, both of these documents – and the *Faro Convention* in particular – were produced at the cusp of what is now commonly referred to as the 'revolution of the social web', which from the early 2000s saw the rise of the global compendium Wikipedia (launched in 2001) and the establishment of numerous social content-sharing online platforms such as Flickr (2004), YouTube (2005) and Facebook (global release in 2005).

Furthermore, terms such as 'dialogue', 'intercultural' and 'diversity' do not feature in the key documents that outline the scope and purpose of the digitisation of heritage in Europe, such as the 2006 and 2011 editions of the *Commission's Recommendation on the Digitisation and Online Accessibility of Cultural Material and Digital Preservation* (2006, 2011) and the mission statement of the European digital heritage platform *Europeana* (launched in 2008).[1] Indeed, it is noticeable that in the most recent *New European Agenda for Culture* (European Commission 2008) (which was the first European Agenda for Culture to mention impact of the digital on culture), references to heritage's potential in creating 'dialogue' or 'intercultural dialogue' have been dropped altogether, to be replaced instead by an emphasis on 'nurturing peaceful relations' (p. 7) between nations. However, 'cultural diversity' holds a central position in the *Recommendation of the Committee of Ministers to Member States on the Internet of Citizens* (2016) – indeed, the latter reconfirms full respect for the 2005 UNESCO *Convention on the Protection and Promotion of the Diversity of Cultural Expressions*. All of these documents maintain a clear emphasis on increasing access to heritage resources in Europe or individuals and communities through 'the permanent preservation of all relevant human creative expression for future generations through mass digitisation programmes' (ibid.); in the case of *Europeana*, this can be further achieved through a culture of openness and collaboration among all stakeholders. In a similar vein, the overarching *Digital Agenda for Europe* (Council of Europe, 2010), when it comes to heritage, forgoes any mentions of dialogue and interculturality and emphasises the role of digital infrastructure and tools in increasing accessibility to European heritage through digitisation, as well as promoting cultural and creative diversity through pluralism in the media and greater opportunities for the creative expression of individuals.

A sense of disconnect between the individual agendas that outline dialogue, heritage and digital practices in a global context also prevails in UNESCO documents. In the case of UNESCO, emphasis on the creation of suitable frameworks for the digitisation and preservation of digital cultural assets for future 'access' is also the focus of relevant declarations, such as UNESCO/UBC's Vancouver Declaration on *The Memory of the World in the Digital Age: Digitization and Preservation* (2012) and the *Recommendation concerning the Protection and Promotion of Museums and Collections, their Diversity and their Role in Society* (UNESCO, 2015). For example, the latter affirms the role of museums as 'key spaces' for dialogue rather than 'merely places where our common heritage is preserved' (ibid., p. 5); however, when it comes to the role of the digital, the emphasis is on 'technologies' and their role in the 'preservation, study, creation and transmission of heritage and related knowledge' (ibid., p. 9). Furthermore, a recent UNESCO survey that looked at the ways intercultural dialogue is understood and operationalised by its member states (UNESCO, 2017) also utilises a limiting interpretation of the digital as 'new technologies' and 'tools'. According to the survey, these new technologies, on the one hand, enable the sharing and creation of new cultural expressions, while on the other hand, can be used to undermine social inclusion and become a vehicle for hate speech (ibid., p. 8). Awareness of the use of social media for these negative purposes is increasing, for example, with the United Nations' investigation of the recent use of Facebook to promote racial hatred against minority groups in Myanmar (BBC Trending, 2018). However, it is worth noting that respondents to the survey also cited 'the significant rise in the use of social media as a means to enhance civil society voices and foster inclusive participation' (UNESCO, 2017, p. 8).

These initial observations of the language used in the official documents that inform policy and practice in Europe around heritage, dialogue and digital practices suggest that language around digital is still quite slippery: the documents discussed earlier inseparably use terms such as 'new and emerging technologies', 'ICT', 'media', 'the Internet', 'digital media', 'social media' and 'virtual spaces' to refer to a set of tools, platforms or infrastructures that use digital technology. Although all of these documents outline or recommend ways to use these tools for primarily heritage preservation and dissemination purposes, they apply very limited or no attention to the potential dialogic capacities of these tools and the practices they engender for heritage. This is in contradiction to the significant dialogic turn in the heritage and culture-related documents. As many people's everyday affairs, interactions and dialogues progressively take place on digital platforms and

12 *Areti Galani et al.*

rely on digital technology to come to fruition, and as museums and heritage sites are continuously affirmed as spaces for intercultural dialogue for social cohesion and peace in Europe, it is now imperative to explore how these assemblages of digital, dialogic and heritage practices interface.

This chapter attempts to articulate a productive framing of how museological, dialogic and digital practices come together in the European context by drawing attention to the tensions that arise from policy, theory and practice in this field. The chapter interweaves positions and assumptions expressed in relevant European policy documents with museological and philosophical discourse related to dialogue and characteristics of digital culture. For this purpose, we borrow concepts from key thinkers on dialogue such as Bakhtin and Levinas to debate two interrelated aspects: *the conceptualisations of alterity/otherness within heritage in digital culture* and *the articulation of European heritage institutions as neutral spaces for dialogue*. In this respect, the chapter aims to critically engage with two questions and their implications for heritage institutions: (a) who is the dialogue about heritage with, and (b) where (and how) does it take place within the realm of digital culture? The chapter concludes by reflecting on how the dialogic notions of responsibility and answerability can help us to think about ways forward for European heritage institutions in the digital public sphere and their ability to engage with it as a place for dialogue. This is a necessarily selective account as a means for opening a conversation rather than providing definitive positions in this field. In this respect, this chapter maintains a dialogic stance towards Chapters 3, 4 and 5, which provide focused treatments of key ideas and practices related to the topic.

Definitions and key terms

In seeking to respond to some of the themes laid out earlier, it is necessary to provide a definitional background for the key terms used within this chapter. We acknowledge that terms such as 'cultural heritage' (and 'European heritage'), 'dialogue' and 'digital practices' have received significant attention by philosophers, theorists and other disciplinary researchers over a long period of time; complex discourses are in place for all three fields. This section, therefore, aims to highlight the aspects of these discourses that help us to build a roadmap for understanding how practices that involve European heritage, dialogue and digital technologies and platforms come to be realised by European heritage institutions and their publics.

Cultural heritage, interculturalism

It is incontrovertible that terms such as 'cultural heritage' have now taken on an almost common-sense definition both across the academic and

Digital and dialogic heritage practices 13

political literature and, as covered by the *Faro Convention* (Council of Europe, 2005), can be understood to refer to 'a group of resources inherited from the past which people identify [...] as a reflection and expression of their constantly evolving values, beliefs, knowledge and traditions' (online, Article 2). Such a definition does, by and large, correspond with the academic literature in this area, where 'cultural heritage' is described as 'a set of values and meanings' (Smith, 2006, p. 11) and is understood by bodies like ICOMOS (International Council on Monuments and Sites) to encapsulate both material and immaterial forces. Although some of the policies related to digital heritage align with this definition of heritage by subscribing to UNESCO's 2005 *Convention on the Protection and Promotion of the Diversity of Cultural Expressions*, the emphasis is more than often on the more traditional definition of heritage as primarily consisting of tangible collections and heritage assets, the cultural, creative and economic value of which can be unlocked through mass digitisation.

The European Union (EU) has been somewhat slower than individual national governments to recognise the power invested in the values associated with cultural heritage; a fact that Tuuli Lähdesmäki (2017) notes is evident in the outpouring of policy documents and briefings on cultural heritage that followed the initial *Faro Convention*. A consequence of this sudden slew of culture-related policy has been, according to Christopher Gordon (2010), an 'often inappropriate elision of "arts/heritage" and "culture" found in documents published by EU', which he acknowledges is 'one of the more obvious sources of confusion in a policy context' (p. 103). Certainly, whilst the early history of the EU was characterised by a top-down push towards fostering a common European identity (Sassatelli, 2002), the strategic underpinnings of this were, more often than not, framed through a common cultural heritage in particular, which the European Commission believed had the power to create 'communality and feeling[s] of belonging among the citizens in the EU' (Lähdesmäki, 2014, p. 402; see also Calligaro, 2014). Therefore, schemes such as the *European Agenda for Culture*, whilst broad in their remit, very often specifically implicate the heritage sector, leading to some of the confusion around how culture is defined and understood within these documents. For the purposes of this chapter, whilst attempts have been made to distinguish between policies that address cultural heritage specifically, and the more sociologically oriented interpretations of culture, some allowance must be made for a crossover between the two in our analysis of the European context.

Regardless of its precise definition, there is a consensus in heritage studies that 'heritage' is understood and experienced through practices of inclusion and exclusion that often assign homogenising values to diverse histories, cultural expressions and their material evidence. According to Smith (2006), these practices give rise and maintain a dominant way of

14 *Areti Galani et al.*

perceiving heritage through what she terms the 'Authorised Heritage Discourse' (AHD). Reflecting on the capacity of heritage to accommodate both diverse and alternative forms of identity in Europe, Macdonald (2013) asks the question: 'can and should a "European heritage" be identified that transcends national and other diversities within Europe?" (p. 162). Macdonald subsequently develops the argument for both a transcultural and a transnational European heritage, which is particularly relevant to the notion of dialogue and the dialogic practices examined in this volume. Mason (2013) similarly argues that national and transnational understandings of heritage can coexist simultaneously and can be understood through a framework of situated cosmopolitanism. Although Smith, Macdonald and Mason approach heritage from different angles, they have in common a preoccupation with the practices that underpin our understandings of heritage; for example, Smith (2006) emphasises the role of heritage practices, such as listing schemes and cultural policies, in maintaining AHD. It is essential to pay attention to the emergence of practices among heritage professionals in relation to the policies developed by supranational bodies such as the European Commission in order to understand Lähdesmäki's (2012) observation that in European policies, culture and heritage have often been regarded as tools for advancing the EU's political project, rather than multilayered, complex and contested domains in their own right.

Such framings are present in the *White Paper on ICD*, where cultural heritage is described as a space in which dialogue between divided communities takes place by 'offer[ing] scope for mutual recognition by individuals from diverse backgrounds' (Council of Europe, 2008, p. 33). Undoubtedly, dialogue *per se* is ubiquitous in European Commission's practices – as indicated by current schemes such as *Citizens' Dialogues* (public debates with European Commissioners and other EU decision-makers), *Social Dialogue* (between the representatives of the European trade unions and employers' organisations) and *Structured Dialogue* (between young people and decision-makers in Europe). In these cases, dialogue is seen as a means to delivering the democratic and participatory promise of EU by enabling multiple and diverse stakeholders to shape the decision making of the European Commission. On the other hand, distinctly from the more operational approaches to dialogue, intercultural dialogue (ICD) is specifically articulated as 'a forward-looking model for managing cultural diversity' (Council of Europe, 2008, p. 4) as a means for realising European identity; in turn, the latter is expected to be grounded on 'shared fundamental values, respect for common heritage and cultural diversity as well as respect for the equal dignity of every individual' (ibid.). Intercultural dialogue, therefore, is tasked with negotiating the coexistence of commonality and diversity within individuals, groups and nations, or as Näss (2010) puts it, 'the

Digital and dialogic heritage practices 15

line between acceptable diversity and unacceptable difference' (online) in Europe. It is this emphasis on the responsibility of the people of Europe (and the EU member states) to manage otherness, and the conceptualisations of otherness, as articulated by the *White Paper on ICD*, that we aim to connect to philosophical and museological preoccupations with dialogue, *per se*, in the European context.

Dialogue and the 'dialogic museum'

As observed by Stanley Deetz and Jennifer Simpson (2004), some of the most formative work on Western articulations of dialogue emerged in the early twentieth century, corresponding with the development of several philosophical turns; it could be broadly categorised according to the perspectives of liberal humanists, critical hermeneutics and postmodernists. Others, including Deetz and Simpson, have already done the work of unpacking the various scholarly contributions made during this period (Anderson, Baxter and Cissna, 2004; Stewart, Zediker and Black, 2004; Kögler, 2014). This chapter does not aim to provide a comprehensive account of the philosophical approaches to dialogue, but rather focuses on the elements of these approaches that help us understand the position of dialogue in relation to heritage and digital practices. To this end, we draw on writings by Levinas and Bakhtin from the last three quarters of the twentieth century, and their applications in the museological and heritage context. Often regarded as the forebears of much of the current work on dialogue, whether in relation to education (Rule, 2013; Wegerif, 2008), critical psychology (Boe *et al.*, 2013) or philosophy (Erdinast-Vulcan, 2008; Oliver, 2001), the most commonly cited aspects of Bakhtin's and Levinas's work tend to focus on their shared commitment to exploring the subjectivities that precede dialogue and their impact on the formation of a 'new' ethics of responsibility. Their approach to the central themes of alterity and otherness, and their positioning in relation to the role of responsibility and answerability provide, we argue, a productive bridge between the calls articulated in the EU policies on intercultural dialogue and cultural heritage, and the challenges of museological practice in this context.

Although not directly referencing Bakhtin and Levinas, many of the ideas they explored can be directly seen in the museological literature of recent years. For example, within museological practice, the notion of the dialogic museum as articulated by Tchen (1992) highlighted that a dialogue-driven museum practice had the capacity to make the Chinatown History Museum 'a more resonant and responsible history centre' (p. 291) towards improving New York and the community at large; it also acknowledged that the identity of Chinese residents in New York had been 'formed by many layers of influences', which means that 'the self is intricately tied to "others"' (p. 294). Furthermore, in his provocation statement for the 2011 ICOFOM annual meeting on the topic of '[t]he dialogic museum and the visitor experience', Jacobi (2011) advocates the need for museums to enable conscious and explicit modes of dialogue rather than relying on the inherent dialogical nature of the very act of the production of content for the communication tools and the education documents of the museum (p. 18). While Harris (2011) in the same forum refers to Bakhtin to clarify that the binary 'one-to-one dialogue', that is, the dialogue between a museum and its visitors, is 'a very limiting understanding of dialogism', as it maintains the assumption of the museums' cultural privilege, stemming from its 'old authority and power' as a propagator of 'national citizenry' and 'bourgeois taste' (pp. 9–10).

In many respects, the terms 'dialogic' and/or 'participatory museum' – terms that are further explored in Chapters 3 and 4 of this volume – have come to encompass a significant variety and volume of museological practices that are preoccupied with the relationship between heritage institutions and communities, as well as the deployment of diverse modes of participation and exchange between the two. However, Boast (2011), in his critique of Clifford's notion of the 'museum as a contact zone', warns his readers against an uncritical acceptance of the intentions, promise and, ultimately, effect of these participatory practices and 'cross-cultural dialogues'. The springboard of his cautionary critique is not just the inherent asymmetry of the communicative practices between a valorising institution and its communities but also 'the fundamental asymmetries, appropriations and biases' (Boast, 2011, p. 67) that underpin several Western heritage institutions due to their colonial genesis.

The transformative power of digital?

It appears as if this call for a radical re-thinking of heritage institutions, and the way they position themselves in relation to their audiences and community stakeholders, pushes theorists and policy makers alike to champion the potential transformative power of digital technology, especially that of online platforms and digitisation techniques. For example, the section on *Digital Cultural Heritage* policy on the website of the *European Digital Single Market Strategy* proclaims that 'cultural heritage breathes a new life with digital technologies and the internet' (European Commission, n.d.). However, we share Parry's (2005) still-valid concern that many institutions and, we add, policy makers, adopt a techno-deterministic approach to digital heritage presuming that technology itself can somehow do the radical re-rethinking and lead to transformation of heritage institutions. This approach does not appear to take into consideration the socially and culturally constructed nature of digital technologies and their practices of use. An example of this somewhat uncritical attribution of agency is the ultimately utopian idea, if taken literally, that technology can give 'new life' to heritage, as seen in the earlier quotation. However, it is left unclear who or what will determine what this new life is going to be.

Van den Akker and Legêne's (2016) analysis of technological interventions in museums and cultural spaces also highlights the positive transformative nature of technology to challenge pre-existing hegemonies. They argue that a key change impacting museums in digital culture is the new 'knowledge infrastructure' of on-site and online museums that does not only redefine 'what we take to be objects and collections' but also 'may challenge existing power relations and offer opportunities for new forms of self-representation and communication' (p. 8). In this new context, 'information technology strengthens the ease with which master narratives are broken open, and it may multiply the possible relations between art and artefacts from different times and places, both on-site and online' (ibid.) while museums 'work *with* rather *for* their community' (ibid., p. 9).

Gere offers a parallel suggestion for how digital technologies can reshape relationships between museums and their communities. Drawing on Clifford's idea of the 'contact zone', Gere (1997) suggests that the idea of the 'contact zone' could be interpreted to conceptualise the museum's relations with its communities in terms of a de-centralised network, rather than the core (museum) and periphery (communities) paradigm most commonly utilised in museum scholarship (Nightingale, 2009). However, Gere warns us that although digital technologies, and specifically the Internet, can provide a useful way to re-imagine the museum, its promise for a symmetrical and reciprocal mode of communication is not straightforward. Instead, the Internet – like the museum – is defined by asymmetry in patterns of access and use that 'are not limited to the practical' (ibid., p. 65). These asymmetries can be seen as both a challenge and an opportunity for the museum; for example, in the case of digital objects, Srinivasan *et al.* (2010) highlight their positive potential for community work as 'they can carry a multitude of complex references to the original physical object, while being decoupled from its dominant institutional account' (p. 747).

What is evident from this exploration of the terms underpinning this chapter is an often-utopian approach to the articulation of the potential of both heritage and digital technologies for intercultural exchange and dialogue. To some extent, this reflects the fact that at its heart, Europe, and more particularly the European Union (EU), is a fundamentally utopian construction. Borne out of a period of intense international conflict and designed to act as a shield for European nations against future disputes between nations and across continents, the creation of the EU also signified the attempted creation of a new imaginative community (Toplak and Sumi, 2012). Admittedly, the cultural dynamics of this imagined community did not become foundational to the EU project until the 1980s with the establishment of the *European City of Culture* initiative, a direct consequence, Monica Sassatelli (2002) argues, of the realisation that 'legal and economic integration alone will not create a united Europe' (p. 435). In this context, heritage was swiftly identified as a key *locus* for European identity and by 1987, Christopher Gordon (2010) suggests, was being identified by the European Commission as 'a prerequisite for solidarity' (p. 102). This emphasis on harmony and solidarity also underpins references made within European policy documents (such as the *White Paper on IDC*) to digital platforms as intrinsically 'open' spaces, an idea that is often accompanied by the under-examined assumption that such openness is an automatic precursor for dialogue. The normative nature of this assumption is the key issue when thinking about the potential of digital heritage. Whilst this approach can be seen as insufficiently critical, it is very much in keeping with other EU policy documents and initiatives that frame dialogue as the necessary transition into an ideal European society, one which is perhaps based on an overly optimistic understanding of people's willingness to engage across cultural and social divides in the first place. How this societal vision is reinforced through EU policies and how this, in turn, is interpreted and actualised on the ground by heritage sector workers is fundamental for understanding the way that digital dialogues coalesce with the cultural sector. The following two sections explore two key aspects of dialogue that are pertinent to museological practice and policy in Europe: *the notion of alterity and/or otherness* and *the conceptualisation of the dialogic space in a networked society*. Subsequently, the discussion section asks whether museums in Europe have the responsibility to enable and participate in dialogue in digital culture, what form this might take, under which conditions and to what end.

Alterity and otherness in relation to dialogue

As outlined earlier, the concept of dialogue in both a philosophical and practical sense necessarily involves a self and an other. It thereby necessitates an encounter with *difference* and *otherness*, which is also in the heart of the European Commission's preoccupations with intercultural dialogue, as also discussed earlier. Difference and otherness coexist in the philosophical and anthropological term 'alterity', which the *Oxford English Dictionary* defines as 'the state of being other or different'. In this respect, engaging with alterity through intercultural dialogue can also be taken to point towards a conscious engagement with dissimilarity and distinction within the European cultural context. However, a review of the critical responses

(Näss, 2010; Phipps, 2014) to the various policy documents put forward by the European Union (EU) on issues of intercultural dialogue quickly shows that the translation of the principles underpinning intercultural dialogue into policy is far from smooth, precisely because of the darker side of European heritage relating to slavery, colonialism, genocide, war, displacement of peoples and institutionalised and everyday racism. Awareness of such issues is less obvious in the EU's own literature, although the *Report on the Role of Public Arts and Cultural Institutions in the Promotion of Cultural Diversity and Intercultural Dialogue* (European Union, 2014) does offer some reflection on the role that conflict can play in dialogue:

> Intercultural dialogue therefore consists of both and agreement and a disagreement with each other, a consensus and dissent between expressions.
>
> (p. 10)
>
> Intercultural dialogue has the possibility to combat the limits of the universalism of human rights that does not take into account cultural differences, and the limits of multiculturalism, which gives them a social and political recognition but at the same time creates risks of division.
>
> (p. 11)

For example, in the EU's flagship *White Paper on ICD*, which at the time of its publication attracted heavy criticism from activists and academics alike, dialogue is, as Robert Aman (2012) has highlighted, conceived of as operating through a dualistic relationship between the EU and its immigrant 'others'; in this context, traits identified as 'European' are implicitly constructed along colonialist and racial lines. Such criticisms are reinforced by Alison Phipps (2014, p. 112), who argues that the aforementioned policy paper fundamentally fixes the inequalities produced by the EU's relationship to its racial 'others' by redirecting attention onto 'perceptions of cultural difference', thereby absolving the EU of any of the structural violence historically inflicted on colonial communities by many European countries. A similarly restrictive understanding of this relationship between the EU and its others also percolates through some of the core documentation on cultural heritage such as the *Faro Convention*, where the stress that is placed on cultivating a 'common heritage of Europe' (Council of Europe, 2005) presumes a European identity formed in isolation from the rest of the non-Western world, a thesis with which decolonial scholars such as Gurminder Bhambra (2016) and Walter Mignolo (2002) take explicit issue. Although European policy scholars (e.g. Calligaro, 2014; Agustín, 2012) argue that in the *White Paper on ICD*, the distinctive emphasis on common culture and heritage, which defined earlier cultural policies of the European Commission, is diluted (Agustín, 2012) and, instead, has given way to a set of 'shared values' that will hold European diversity together (Calligaro, 2014, p. 78), the lack of explicit acknowledgement in this document of the underlying historic tensions defining Europe's diversity remains.

Such an approach to difference stands in stark contrast to Bakhtin's and Levinas's approaches to alterity which, whilst divergent on many key points, remains absolute about the mutual dependency that exists between the subject and the other of dialogue. For Levinas in particular, this relationship is a deeply protean one, in which the subject comes into being only through their encounter with the other who they are compelled to respond to (Kögler, 2005); Bakhtin too stresses the importance of difference as 'a form of connection' (Sidorkin, 2002, p. 85), which Erdinast-Vulcan (2008) suggests is based on an understanding of the dialogic relationship as one of continuous, reciprocal exchange between subject and other. Bhambra (2016), reflecting specifically on how diverse policies (in the UK and elsewhere) approach the relationship between immigration and multiculturalism in Europe, strongly argues that one of the unresolved issues of diversity in Europe in the context of increased im/migrations is that in these policies, 'multicultural others are not seen as constitutive of Europe's own self-understanding' (p. 188).

For those working in, or on, heritage, the mis-recognition of the multicultural other as part of self very often starts with the subtle elision between 'dialogic' and 'community' work. As discussed in the previous section, the dialogic turn in museum practice has been triggered by concerns with community work; moreover, as discussed in Chapter 3 of this volume, dialogue as a structured activity often falls within the remit of museum education, outreach staff or both. Within the European context, such an elision between the work of dialogue and that of community mirrors the instrumentalism that features in the *White Paper on ICD*, where dialogue is conceived of as a tool for mediating community relations and resolving issues related to multicultural conflict, rather than a continuous and natural part of societal interaction as a whole. This slippage between dialogue and community work also becomes part of the restrictive casting of multicultural others. As Laurajane Smith and Emma Waterton (2010) have argued, this work within heritage often revolves around the artificial construction of a 'seemingly homogenous collective defined by ethnicity, class, education or religion' that 'reinforce[s] presumed differences between the white, middle classes and "the rest"' (p. 5). Such an approach to community engagement, which presumes monologic difference as its starting point for dialogue, is in concerted opposition to the more philosophical understandings of the ideal conditions for dialogue which should, as the Brazilian philosopher of critical pedagogy Paulo Freire (2005) argues, be a more reflexive 'epistemological

Digital and dialogic heritage practices 21

relationship' between self, and cannot, he continues, 'occur between those who want to name the world and those who do not wish this naming' (p. 86). Whilst the aforementioned critiques suggest that a more limited approach to the other of the dialogic process may be somewhat embedded in museological practice at the moment, it is also frequently asserted that digital technologies can help to shift some of these barriers. Indeed, in the early days of writing about the Internet, digital networks were regarded as somewhat utopic spaces in which community could transcend the usual geographic, cultural or social boundaries (Rheingold, 2000). It is not a coincidence, we argue, that some of the bolder claims about the capacity of digital technologies to address the challenges of otherness in the heritage sector in Europe and elsewhere relate to community-oriented projects that utilise participatory media and sharing platforms often associated with Web 2.0 – it is worth noting though that critical discussion on how digital heritage community practices specifically advance epistemological understandings of alterity in Europe is very limited. The capacity afforded by digital technologies to document, disseminate, store and provide access to cultural content (often in real time) has been interpreted by researchers as a catalyst for what Thornton (2007) calls 'civic pluralism' in virtual heritage, referring to digital heritage projects in Canada that enable diverse users to contribute their memories and local history online displays within a single digital platform hosted by CHIN (Canadian Heritage Information Network). Elsewhere, also in relation to online community memory projects, Affleck and Kvan (2008) see the opportunity of sharing of individuals' stories and memories online as the distinctive contribution of digital technology to the realisation of a 'discursive interpretation' of heritage, while Simon (2012) suggests that particular forms of 'remembering together' in online platforms may 'incorporate an interactive regard for the non-equivalent, singularity of others, particularly those who have been subjected to the violence of injustice' (p. 93). The latter is demonstrated in a poignant example of impromptu interreligious dialogue enabled by Facebook (Illman, 2011) in Turku, Finland, in 2010. In the unfortunate event of the vandalism of the Vietnamese Buddhist temple in Turku, an informal solidarity group on Facebook was soon created, which, according to Illman, 'offered a forum where minority groups such as Buddhists, neo-pagans, and Muslims could engage in dialogue with one another without the mediation of either the state or the Lutheran church' (ibid., p. 51), demonstrating the capacity of social media platforms to enable the fluid assembling and re-configuration of otherness in response to common issues of concerns. All of the authors cited here, however, also critically reflect on the limitations of these technologies to currently fully deliver on their potential to re-configure already cemented understandings of alterity or to move, in the case of online memory work, beyond the interests of the individuals.

22 *Areti Galani et al.*

The proliferation of examples and case studies in the literature like the ones mentioned here suggests that heritage and cultural practices that are preoccupied with alterity increasingly inhabit dialogic spaces as part of a broader digital public sphere, which is not limited to traditional heritage institutions. How heritage institutions negotiate alterity and new configurations of dialogic spaces in this digital public sphere and to what extent intercultural dialogue and heritage change as a result of this negotiation is the focus of the next section.

How heritage is transformed by the digital public sphere

Policy documents, heritage literature and practice have firmly presented the physical space of the museum as a fitting place for intercultural dialogue (Bodo, Gibbs and Sani, 2009). Dialogic space in the actual museum environment is materialised either through its exhibitions or the programming of specific dialogue-oriented activities, which bring diverse communities together. This often aligns with a perception among museum workers that dialogue is a face-to-face activity, as discussed by Arrigoni and Galani in Chapter 3 of this volume. Delgado (2009, p. 9), Bodo (2009, p. 22) and Simone (2009, p. 32), in their exploration of intercultural projects in European heritage and cultural institutions, further utilise Homi Bhabha's concept of the 'third space' to articulate dialogic space in terms of not just bricks and mortar but also a set of potentialities, where diverse communities can encounter each other through active exploration, and the generation of new knowledge and experiences. They do not, however, provide further reflection on how museum dialogic spaces may be shaped by digital technologies and platforms.

However, as already mentioned earlier in this chapter, museums are progressively conceptualised not as institutions that are bound by their walls but as networks, rhizomes or both; they also inherently inhabit a networked society. On this issue, Innocenti (2014) provided a thorough and persuasive investigation of European cultural heritage and its memory institutions as nodes in a progressively networked culture and society. For the purpose of this chapter, we understand network society as 'a social formation with an infrastructure of social and media networks enabling its prime mode of organisation at all levels (individual, group/organisational and societal)' (van Dijk, 2006, p. 20). In this new context, intercultural dialogue around and through heritage also requires a new articulation.

Although the idea of the museum as a platform initially surfaced in the early 2000s (Dietz *et al.*, 2003), that is, predating the social web, it was Proctor (n.d.) in the late 2000s who provided, for its time, an avant-garde proposition of the museum as a 'distributed network'. As Proctor vividly describes, 'in the museum as distributed network, content and experience creation resembles atoms coming together and reforming on new platforms to create new molecules, or "choose your own ending" adventure stories' (ibid., online). In this context, digital technologies are highlighted as enablers of cooperation between organisations and dissemination of cultural assets in different scales, local, national, global and transnational contexts which, as Nuria Sanz (2018) asserts, 'in a global world, often overlap' (p. 46). This networked reality is significant in relation to the role of European museums as dialogic spaces, as it also powers the active de-centralisation of truth and its re-conceptualisation as constantly emergent, relational and intertextual. As Proctor writes:

> Truth, rather than being disseminated outwards from a centre point, is discovered in its intersections and interstices, through the (sometimes surprising) juxtapositions that can happen when experiences are assembled collaboratively along the many-branched paths of a rhizome.
> (n.d., online)

Undoubtedly, digital networks alter the way many people engage with each other and with 'things'. Sunstein (2004) explains that a pertinent characteristic of established digital networks is the 'dramatic increase in individual control over content along with a corresponding decrease in the power of general-interest intermediaries, including newspapers, magazines, and broadcasters' (p. 58). A recent European report on the promotion of culture via digital means also suggests:

> With the growing importance of search engines, mobile applications, digital distribution platforms and channels, the role of cultural institutions in the value chain has changed, and continues to do so. Cultural institutions are still trusted sources of digital information and provide valuable digital products and services, but they are seldom the sole owners of the whole information life cycle from production to consumption, use and possible re-use or the sole owners of the stream from the institution to the user. Users co-produce, tailor and re-use the content to better serve their needs for self-expression, community building, learning and fun.
> (Council of European Union, 2017, p. 26)

This means that despite the apparent infinite connectivity and the promise for serendipity on digital platforms, individuals nowadays have the capacity to accurately filter the content they encounter to match with their interests and points of view, a phenomenon commonly referred to as the 'echo chamber' or 'filter bubble'. It is within this context that the *silencing* of the other becomes a very real possibility; a concern which has become a mainstream political issue in the last few years. By contrast, bodies such as public service broadcasters in democratic societies which intentionally gather and present multiple perspectives online can provide a more pluralistic and heterogenous set of information and perspectives. As Sunstein (2004) indicates, this is not to argue that general-interest intermediaries – and we can include several heritage institutions in this category – do not have their own 'limitations and biases' but to highlight that 'people who rely on such intermediaries experience a range of chance encounters with diverse others, as well as exposure to material they did not specifically choose' (ibid.).

This emphasis on individuation in online communications raises real concerns around the fragmentation of culture within digital networks 'as infinitesimal differentiations based especially on political interests, taste cultures and advertising-driven demographic segments drive a seemingly exponential "niching" of online fora' (Goode, 2010, p. 530) – although opposing views are also prevalent in this field (e.g. Dahlberg, 2007). Inevitably, it also raises the question of how we can conceptualise the position of heritage and intercultural dialogue in the digital public sphere or spheres. Van Dijk (2006), for example, promotes a more balanced view on the matter; he indicates that relations in network society 'are ever more realised by a combination of social and media networks', in which 'offline and online communication become more and more combined leading to the emergence of a *mosaic*-like public sphere rather than a fragmented one' (p. 39, italics in the original). Van Dijk speculates that this emerging form of public sphere will comprise 'overlapping spheres that will keep common denominators' (ibid.).

This optimistic approach to the potentialities of digital platforms is also echoed by Nuria Sanz's (2018) discussion of heritage. Sanz argues:

> [D]espite the visible growth of intolerance and anti-intellectualism in different parts of the globe, museums, with their inclusive and democratic vocations and their cosmopolitan interests, constitute a great opportunity to continue disseminating the message of the importance of plurality and diversity in the contemporary world.
>
> (p. 52)

While we would agree in theory, we must ask what position heritage and cultural institutions will take in this new fluid and layered public sphere. From a positive and optimistic perspective, the common and shared heritage advocated by the EU policies could operate as the common denominator among diverse but overlapping public spheres – an example of this is provided by Farrell-Banks in Chapter 5 of this volume. This would require museums to consciously inhabit the digital public sphere and negotiate its de-centralising character by materialising their capacity as distributed spaces for dialogue that transcend both social and technical networks. However, we argue that one of the key steps forward for European museums to achieve this potentiality is to deal with the misconception of dialogic space (both within their premises broadly and online) as neutral.

Networked heritage and the question of neutrality

References to museums as neutral spaces are common both in European policies and EU-funded research (e.g. Bodo, Gibbs and Sani, 2009). For example, a 2008 report on advancing intercultural dialogue within cultural institutions asked how cultural institutions could create 'neutral spaces for intercultural encounters [. . .] where everybody will feel safe, welcome and comfortable' (Council of European Union, 2014, p. 26). On one hand, it could be argued that the value of the online museum or heritage organisation is precisely as a trusted platform on which different perspectives can be brought into contact and alterity can be experienced. Given the increasing tendency for people to seek out and engage only with content online that reflects their own perspectives (the filter bubble or echo chamber effect described earlier), it might be argued that the museum or heritage organisation's ability to be a genuine broadcaster of views rather than narrowcaster is its most valuable asset.

However, neutrality is not, as the political theorist Iris Marion Young (1997) articulates, a particularly useful starting point for dialogue; dialogue, she argues, emerges from more asymmetrical moral and social relations between people and, crucially, it requires individuals to be transparent about their positions for dialogue to be effective. An important distinction here is whether we are discussing individuals holding views and being transparent online about their positionality, or the museum or heritage organisation as an institution which – it is commonly said – can give space to the views of multiple individuals' perspectives while not endorsing a single viewpoint. This is, itself, an enormous topic of debate at present in museological circles. We are thinking here of online campaigns such as 'Museums are not neutral' and those who argue that museums always inevitably adopt a position (e.g. given their historic involvement in colonialism and the acquisition of cultural property in times of war) so that neutrality is not a possibility. At the same time, the opposite point of view is that museums should seek to remain objective and present multiple perspectives for the public to make their own judgements. This can be summarised in the idea of the museum as a platform which hosts a range of voices and enables them to be heard in, and by, the public. This idea was encapsulated by Tony Bennett as far back as 1995 in *The Birth of the Museum*, where he wrote:

> [I]t is imperative that the role of curator be shifted away from that of the source of an expertise whose function is to organize a representation claiming the status of knowledge and towards that of the possessor of a technical competence whose function is to assist groups outside the museum to use its resources to make authored statements within in it.
>
> (Bennett, 1995, pp. 103–104)

The point here is that neutrality is not a precondition for polyvocality; a commitment to the latter, however, would require cultural institutions to reflect on their own positionality and willingness to play the part as described by Bennett.

Similarly, we recognise that scholars of digital culture have already argued that the Internet, and digital technologies at large, cannot be viewed as a neutral platform for exchange and debate, but are seen to actively shape debates through the technological limits and affordances built into its platforms (Graves, 2007; Papacharissi, 2002). Like their physical counterparts, museum and heritage organisations online will need to consider the limits of the debates and viewpoints they would be prepared to host if they were to really function as a platform. For example, institutions will need to consider the ethical and legal nature of their position if drawn into online debates about contentious objects. In an era of 'fake news', they will also need to consider with renewed urgency what position they will adopt around ideas of truth, opinion, facts, interpretation and personal perspective. Such concerns are made apparent in Farrell-Banks's (Chapter 5) contribution to this volume, in which he explores the role that the use of Twitter plays in fuelling right-wing populism's appropriations online of *Magna Carta*.

Despite these significant issues, we observe that several EU policies on intercultural dialogue continue to be optimistic about its ability to cultivate dialogue through digital culture. In one of the few documents to actually make the links between dialogue, culture and the digital explicit – a study carried out for the European Commission on how ICD is understood and operationalised by member states – 'virtual realities' and 'digitalised cultural products' are described as 'play[ing] an important role in fostering intercultural dynamics' and 'new forms of trans-culturalism' within the arts and cultural sector (ERICArts, 2008, p. 30); furthermore, 'virtual environments' as a whole are conceptualised as 'important spaces for intercultural dialogue' (ERICArts, 2008, p. xii), with only passing reference made to their ability to inspire conflict between participants and perpetuate structural inequality. In the recent policies about the role of digital technology

Digital and dialogic heritage practices 27

in culture, some concerns are also expressed; for example, the brief *Final Statement of the 10th Council of Europe Conference of Ministers of Culture* (Council of Europe, 2013) stresses 'the importance of the digital revolution' as 'crucial to the viability of creation and cultural diversity', while also warning about its capacity to defuse culture and to 'influence strongly the cultural environment' (p. 2). Furthermore, the *Recommendation of the Committee of Ministers to Member States on the Internet of Citizens* (2016), also declares the need to 'exploit' the positive potential of digital culture, 'while safeguarding against related threats such as infringement of privacy, breaches of data security, hate speech or manipulation' (online).

However, the dominant direction of travel in these documents is towards an overly future-oriented articulation of digitisation of culture and development of digital literacies as means to safeguarding cultural diversity, boosting creativity and unlocking financial prosperity. Claims like these appear to sidestep the challenges raised by the utopianism of so-called net neutrality and its contemporary impacts by advocating instead the mass digitisation of 'all *relevant* human creative expression for future generations' (*Recommendation of the Committee of Ministers to member States on the Internet of citizens*, 2016, italics added); hence, addressing the challenges of cultural diversity in the digital public sphere through the promise of profusion of digital cultural assets.

In light, however, of these emerging tensions between neutrality and positionality, selectivity and profusion of digital cultural products and cultural diversity and trans-culturalism, one needs to reflect on (a) what the responsibilities are for cultural institution, (b) whether the discourses around intercultural dialogue and digital heritage are compatible ones and (c) what is at stake.

Heritage organisations and their dialogic responsibilities in the digital public sphere

This chapter so far has focused on the two fundamental characteristics of dialogue that are being reshaped in digital culture: (a) the conceptualisation of, and engagement with, alterity, and (b) the re-definition of the dialogic space afforded by cultural institutions in a networked digital public sphere. In this concluding section, we aim to articulate our reflections on two areas of renewed museum responsibility emerging from the earlier discussion drawing on Bakhtin's and Levinas's notions of answerability and responsibility.

The first area of renewed museum responsibility arises from the policy's emphasis on the value of 'mass digitisation' of European cultural and heritage assets. To be clear, we do not advocate for less urgency and investment on digitisation schemes – these schemes are the lifeline for cultural production in the digital public sphere. Instead, we want to draw attention to the risks in what Alexander Badenoch (2011) defines as a 'moral encoding of the mission of digitisation' in EU's digital strategy, which, he argues, is 'reminiscent of the role of the nineteenth century museum in displaying the progress of the nation-state' (p. 301). This is echoed in Taylor and Gibson's (2017) critique of a common claim in relation to digital heritage that access to digitised collections and materials is itself a means to democratisation. They suggest that what we need to ask is not just whether individual and communities have access but also *what kind* of access they have and whether the power dynamics unravelled in digitisation processes lead to the reproduction of the hegemonic structures already present in museum collections. The implication of their line of argument is whether, inadvertently, profusion of digital cultural assets by long-established (national and supranational) institutions through digitisation will render some of the *less relevant*, and subsequently *less preferable*, forms of heritage even less discoverable.

We argue, however, that in this policy context and the fast-configuring space of the digital public sphere, digitisation should be re-conceptualised as a process, rather than a set of techniques and tools, that allows institutions and communities to engage with the dialogic ethics of answerability in Bakhtin's work. Answerability draws attention to the relational and situated character of being in the world and acknowledges reciprocity as the inherent process through which the self is formed as unique – 'a non-alibi of Being' (Bakhtin, 1993, p. 42). As Murray (2000) explains, in Bakhtin's work, 'the self is called into responsibility by the Other – whose very presence is the originary source of the ethical imperative – and the self retains its freedom of ethical response through its answerability for its actions' (p. 134). For the digitisation of European heritage to overcome the risk expressed earlier by Badenoch, we argue that cultural institutions should engage in a particular balancing act between the urgency for a 'demand-led' (*Recommendation of the Committee of Ministers to Member States on the Internet of Citizens*, 2016) approach to access to cultural heritage, advocated by the policy, and the interpretation of access, not as a call for delivering digitised assets for intercultural dialogue, but as a means for delivering a dialogic ethos *per se*. The latter requires cultural institutions and supranational bodies, like the EU, to embed dialogue between institutions, individuals and communities in digital heritage policies as a process for decision-making rather than as the outcome of it.

The second area of renewed responsibility for heritage institutions arises from their re-location in the context of the digital public sphere and the need for them to re-think the boundaries of the dialogic spaces they wish

Digital and dialogic heritage practices 29

to create, as well as their role in them. In other words, *how far should these sites go in accommodating the zeitgeist of contemporary opinion* and *when, by contrast, should they stop becoming response-able to segments of the public?* In response to this dilemma, Sanz (2018) asserts that within digital network society, 'contradictory and alternative networked institutions and communities should be embraced instead of being rejected or perceived as dysfunctional, and re-interpreted as creative agencies and challenges' (pp. 182–183). She sees this as an opportunity to 'add to an institution's contemporaneity and relevance' but also as an inescapable implication of digital media reality, in which

> it is impossible to insulate a portal from conflictual networks, and those acting within organisations now freely draw from a wide range of digitally-connected networks which always limits the effective hegemonic functionality of old established institutions.
>
> (ibid.)

Such issues are raised in all chapters of this volume and, particularly, in Chapter 5 by Farrell-Banks.

In our view, this conundrum is an opportunity for cultural institutions to reconsider their role as civic institutions within an expanded and fluid digital culture. The *Recommendation of the Committee of Ministers to Member States on the Internet of Citizens* (2016) asserts:

> [D]igital culture's positive potential should be fully exploited in helping build a culture of democracy, democratic citizenship and participation, while safeguarding against related threats such as infringement of privacy, breaches of data security, hate speech or manipulation.

Applying a positive reading to this call, we observe an aspiration within the European Commission to capture a more future-oriented digital civicness, through its redefinition of citizenship away from legalistic frameworks and into a 'general sense' of 'people or persons' that puts a 'human rights approach' at its centre (*Recommendation of the Committee of Ministers to Member States on the Internet of Citizens*, 2016). Similarly, the report prepared by ERICArts (2008) in the materialisation of intercultural dialogue policies in European Union member states maintains:

> [S]uccessful ICD projects are to be found in "shared spaces"; both institutional spaces and non-institutional spaces. Within institutional spaces they are those which strive to ensure equality of participation by all groups at levels of both governance (making decisions) and

management (execution of the project) and which bring the activities of minorities and migrants in from the margins and into mainstream organised spheres. [. . .] Non-institutional spaces such as the neighbourhood, city streets, train stations, public parks, marketplaces etc., but also virtual environments, are important spaces for intercultural dialogue. It can be easier for people to understand how they themselves could become innovators of change, if ICD activities become part of the lived daily life experience rather than a separate activity.

(ERICArts, 2008, p. xii)

However, the suggestion that the museum might re-configure their dialogic space to become a platform for many-to-many communication within and beyond their institutional boundaries (*in-situ* and online) – a broadcast model common in social and other online media (Russo *et al.*, 2008; Carpentier, 2011) – does not mean that we automatically revert to the thesis of heritage as a neutral stage for these interactions. Indeed, although Levinas's subject in dialogue may be somewhat passive in their relation to the other, they are still based on a reactive approach to communication, insofar as they are expected to engage in reflexive change as a result of their encounter with the other. Illman (2011), reflecting on the benefits and the pitfalls of the use of Facebook for interreligious dialogue in Finland in the wake of the vandalism of the Vietnamese Buddhist temple discussed earlier in the chapter, suggests that dialogue in this context is better understood as 'non-indifference rather than reciprocity' (p. 56). In this respect, Illman observes the purpose of the solidarity space on Facebook for those involved seemed to be 'to fight one's own indifference' by offering 'a suitable way to move from indifference to non-indifference' but without going as far as 'acknowledging responsibility or acknowledgement of the asymmetrical relationship between self and other, as Levinas urges' (ibid., pp. 56–57).

The challenge for European cultural institutions is how to negotiate the line from indifference to non-indifference for themselves and their publics, and to decide whether a seemingly institutional disinterestedness and a preoccupation with access and openness applied to digital practices on the basis of pre-existing articulations of the self is still a sustainable position if they wish to become actors in the digital public sphere. The opportunity now is for European cultural institutions to move away from conceptualising the digital public sphere as a space to be filled with assets and one-off encounters with diversity, or as a carrier for dialogue, and towards imagining it as a place in which these institutions can redefine their existing communicative practices and relationships with their communities and experiment with new ones.

Acknowledgements

We would like to thank our colleague Dr Joanne Sayner, who provided feedback on earlier versions of this chapter. This research is carried out as part of the project CoHERE (2016–2019), which has received funding from the European Union Horizon 2020 programme under grant agreement NO 693289.

Note

1 In May 2015, *Europeana* became one of European Commission's Digital Service Infrastructures.

References

Affleck, J. and Kvan, T. (2008) 'A virtual community as the context for discursive interpretation: A role in cultural heritage engagement', *International Journal of Heritage Studies*, 14(3), pp. 268–280.
Agustín, Ó. G. (2012) 'Intercultural dialogue visions of the Council of Europe and the European Commission for a post-multiculturalist era', *Journal of Intercultural Communication*, 29. Available at: http://immi.se/intercultural (Accessed: 7 January 2018).
Aman, R. (2012) 'The EU and the recycling of colonialism: Formation of Europeans through intercultural dialogue', *Educational Philosophy and Theory*, 44(9), pp. 1010–1023.
Anderson, R., Baxter, L. and Cissna, K. (eds.) (2004) *Dialogue: Theorizing difference in communication studies*. London: Sage Publications.
Badenoch, A. (2011) 'Harmonized spaces, dissonant objects, inventing Europe? Mobilizing digital heritage', *Culture Unbound: Journal of Current Cultural Research*, 3(3), pp. 295–315.
Bakhtin, M. M. (1993) *Toward a philosophy of the act* (V. Liapunov and M. Holquist, eds., V. Liapunov, Trans.). Austin, TX: University of Texas Press.
BBC Trending. (2018) 'The country where Facebook posts whipped up hate', *BBC trending going in-depth on social media*. Available at: www.bbc.co.uk/news/blogs-trending-45449938 (Accessed: 7 January 2018).
Bennett, T. (1995) *The birth of the museum*. London: Routledge.
Bhambra, G. (2016) 'Whither Europe? Postcolonial versus neocolonial cosmopolitanism', *Interventions*, 18(2), pp. 187–202.
Boast, R. (2011) 'Neocolonial collaboration: Museum as contact zone revisited', *Museum Anthropology*, 34(1), pp. 56–70.
Bodo, S. (2009) 'The challenge of creating "third spaces" – Guidelines for MAP for ID pilot projects', in Bodo, S., Gibbs, K. and Sani, M. (eds.) (2009), *Museums as places for intercultural dialogue: Selected practices from Europe*. MAP for ID Group, pp. 22–25. Available at: www.ne-mo.org/fileadmin/Dateien/public/service/Handbook_MAPforID_EN.pdf (Accessed: 14 January 2019).

Bodo, S., Gibbs, K. and Sani, M. (eds.). (2009) *Museums as places for intercultural dialogue: Selected practices from Europe*. MAP for ID Group. Available at: www.ne-mo.org/fileadmin/Dateien/public/service/Handbook_MAPforID_EN.pdf (Accessed: 14 January 2019).

Boe, T., Kristofferson, K., Lidbom, P., Lindvig, G., Ulland, D. and Zachariassen, K. (2013) 'Change is an ongoing ethical event: Levinas, Bakhtin and the dialogical dynamics of becoming', *Australian and New Zealand Journal of Family Therapy*, 34(1), pp. 18–31.

Calligaro, O. (2014) 'From "European cultural heritage" to "cultural diversity": The changing core values of European cultural policy', *Politique Européenne*, 45(3), pp. 60–85.

Carpentier, N. (2011) 'Contextualising audience-author convergences: "New" technologies' claims to increased participation, novelty and uniqueness', *Cultural Studies*, 25(4–5), pp. 517–533.

'Commission recommendation of 24 August 2006 on the digitisation and online accessibility of cultural material and digital preservation'. (2006) *Official Journal of the European Union L236*, pp. 28–30. Available at: https://eur-lex.europa.eu/legal-content/EN/TXT/PDF/?uri=CELEX:32006H0585&from=EN (Accessed: 14 January 2019).

'Commission recommendation of 27 October 2011 on the digitisation and online accessibility of cultural material and digital preservation'. (2011) *Official Journal of the European Union L283*, pp. 39–45. Available at: https://eur-lex.europa.eu/LexUriServ/LexUriServ.do?uri=OJ:L:2011:283:0039:0045:EN:PDF (Accessed: 14 January 2019).

Council of Europe. (2005) 'Council of Europe Framework Convention on the value of cultural heritage for society, Faro', *Council of Europe Treaty Series*, 199. Available at: www.coe.int/en/web/conventions/full-list/-/conventions/rms/0900001680083746 (Accessed: 7 January 2019).

Council of Europe. (2008) *White paper on intercultural dialogue: Living together as equals with dignity*. Strasbourg: Council of Europe.

Council of Europe. (2010) *A digital agenda for Europe COM(2010)245*. Brussels: European Commission.

Council of Europe. (2013) *Final statement: 10th council of Europe conference of ministers of culture*. Available at: www.culturalpolicies.net/web/files/241/en/MinConfCult2013_7-EN_def.pdf (Accessed: 14 January 2019).

Council of European Union. (2014) *Report on the role of public arts and cultural institutions in the promotion of cultural diversity and intercultural dialogue*. Luxembourg: Publications Office of the European Union.

Council of European Union. (2017) *Promoting access to culture via digital means: Policies and strategies for audience development*. Luxembourg: Publications Office of the European Union.

Dahlberg, L. (2007) 'Rethinking the fragmentation of the cyberpublic: From consensus to contestation', *New Media & Society*, 9(5), pp. 827–847.

Deetz, S. and Simpson, J. (2004) 'Critical organisational dialogue: Open formation and the Demand of "Otherness"', in Anderson, R., Baxter, L. and Cissna, K.

(eds.), *Dialogue: Theorizing difference in communication studies*. London: Sage Publications, pp. 141–158.
Delgado, E. (2009) 'Museums as spaces of negotiation', in Bodo, S., Gibbs, K. and Sani, M. (eds.) (2009), *Museums as places for intercultural dialogue: Selected practices from Europe*. MAP for ID Group, pp. 8–9. Available at: www.ne-mo.org/fileadmin/Dateien/public/service/Handbook_MAPforID_EN.pdf (Accessed: 14 January 2019).
Dietz, S., Besser, H., Borda, A., Geber, K. and Lévy, P. (2003) *Virtual museum (of Canada): The next generation*. Montreal: Canadian Heritage Information Network (CHIN).
Erdinast-Vulcan, D. (2008) 'Between the face and the voice: Bakhtin meets Levinas', *Continental Philosophy Review*, 41, pp. 43–58.
ERICArts. (2008) *Sharing diversity – National approaches to intercultural dialogue in Europe' report*. Brussels: European Commission.
European Commission. (2008) *A new European agenda for culture*. Available at: https://eur-lex.europa.eu/legal-content/EN/TXT/?qid=1527241001038&uri=COM:2018:267:FIN (Accessed: 14 January 2019).
European Commission. (n.d.) *Digital cultural heritage*. Available at: https://ec.europa.eu/digital-single-market/en/policies/digital-cultural-heritage (Accessed: 7 January 2019).
European Union. (2014) *Report on the role of public arts and cultural institutions in the promotion of cultural diversity and intercultural dialogue*. Available at: http://ec.europa.eu/assets/eac/culture/library/reports/201405-omc-diversity-dialogue_en.pdf (Accessed: 14 January 2019).
Freire, P. (2005) *Pedagogy of the oppressed*. London: Continuum.
Gere, R. (1997) 'Museums, contact zones and the internet', *Proceedings of ICHIM 1997*. Available at: www.museumsandtheweb.com/biblio/museums_contact_zones_and_the_internet_0 (Accessed: 10 January 2019).
Goode, L. (2010) 'Cultural citizenship online: The internet and digital culture', *Citizenship Studies*, 14(5), pp. 527–542.
Gordon, C. (2010) 'Great expectations – The European Union and cultural policy: Fact or fiction?', *International Journal of Cultural Policy*, 16(2), pp. 101–120.
Graves, L. (2007) 'The affordances of blogging: A case study in culture and technological effects', *Journal of Communication Inquiry*, 31(4), pp. 331–346.
Harris, J. (2011) 'Discussion of dialogism', *The Dialogic Museum and the Visitor Experience: ICOFOM Study Series, Issue 40*, pp. 9–10. Available at: http://network.icom.museum/fileadmin/user_upload/minisites/icofom/pdf/ISS%2040_ch_web2.pdf (Accessed: 7 January 2019).
Illman, R. (2011) 'Reciprocity and power in philosophies of dialogue: The burning of a Buddhist temple in Finland', *Studies in Interreligious Dialogue*, 21(1), pp. 46–63.
Innocenti, P. (2014) 'Introduction: Migrating heritage – Experiences of cultural networks and cultural dialogue in Europe', in Innocenti, P. (ed.), *Migrating heritage: Experiences of cultural networks and cultural dialogue in Europe*. Farnham: Ashgate, pp. 1–24.

Jacobi, D. (2011) 'Dialogism in museums', *The Dialogic Museum and the Visitor Experience*: ICOFOM Study Series, Issue 40, pp. 17–18. Available at: http://network.icom.museum/fileadmin/user_upload/minisites/icofom/pdf/ISS%2040_ch_web2.pdf (Accessed: 7 January 2019).

Kögler, H. H. (2005) 'Recognition and difference: The power of perspectives in interpretive dialogue', *Social Identities*, 11(3), pp. 247–269.

Kögler, H. (2014) 'A critique of dialogue in philosophical hermeneutics', *Journal of Dialogue Studies*, 2(1), pp. 47–68.

Lähdesmäki, T. (2012) 'Rhetoric of unity and cultural diversity in the making of European cultural identity', *International Journal of Cultural Policy*, 18(1), pp. 59–75.

Lähdesmäki, T. (2014) 'The EU's explicit and implicit heritage politics', *European Societies*, 16(3), pp. 401–421.

Lähdesmäki, T. (2017) 'Narrativity and intertextuality in the making of a shared European memory', *Journal of Contemporary European Studies*, 25(1), pp. 57–72.

Macdonald, S. (2013) *Memorylands, heritage and identity in Europe today*. Oxon: Routledge.

Mason, R. (2013) 'National museums, globalisation and postnationalism: Imagining a cosmopolitan museology', in Dudley, S. and Message, K. (eds.), *Museum worlds: Advances in research*, 1(1), pp. 40–64.

Mignolo, W. (2002) 'The geopolitics of knowledge and the colonial difference', *South Atlantic Quarterly*, 101(1), pp. 57–96.

Murray, J. W. (2000) 'Bakhtinian answerability and Levinasian responsibility: Forging a fuller dialogical communicative ethics', *Southern Journal of Communication*, 65(2–3), pp. 133–150.

Näss, H. E. (2010) 'The ambiguities of intercultural dialogue: Critical perspectives on the European Union's new agenda for culture', *Journal of Intercultural Communication*, 23. Available at: www.immi.se/intercultural/ (Accessed: 14 January 2019).

Nightingale, E. (2009) 'From the margins to the core: Aims, outcomes, and legacies of the capacity building and cultural ownership project', *Journal of Museum Education*, 34(3), pp. 255–269.

Oliver, K. (2001) *Witnessing: Beyond recognition*. London: University of Minnesota Press.

Papacharissi, Z. (2002) 'The virtual sphere: The internet as a public sphere', *New Media and Society*, 4(1), pp. 9–27.

Parry, R. (2005) 'Digital heritage and the rise of theory in museum computing', *Museum Management and Curatorship*, 20(4), pp. 333–348.

Phipps, A. (2014) '"They are bombing now": "Intercultural dialogue" in times of conflict', *Language and Intercultural Communication*, 14(1), pp. 108–124.

Proctor, N. (n.d.) 'The museum as distributed network, a 21st century model', *Museum I*. Available at: http://museum-id.com/museum-distributed-network-21st-century-model-nancy-proctor/ (Accessed: 14 January 2019).

'Recommendation of the Committee of Ministers to Member States on the Internet of Citizens CM/REC(2016)/2'. (2016) *Council of Europe*. Available at: https://search.coe.int/cm/Pages/result_details.aspx?ObjectId=09000016805c20f4 (Accessed: 14 January 2019).

Rheingold, H. (2000) *The virtual community: Homesteading on the electronic frontier*. London: MIT Press.
Rule, P. (2013) 'Bakhtin and Freire: Dialogue, dialectic and boundary learning', *Educational Philosophy and Theory*, 43, pp. 924–942.
Russo, A., Watkins, J., Kelly, L. and Chan, S. (2008) 'Participatory communication with social media', *Curator*, 51(1), pp. 21–31.
Sanz, N. (ed.). (2018) *U.N.E.S.C.O. – Museums and dialogue between culture*. Available at: http://unesdoc.unesco.org/images/0026/002658/265880m.pdf (Accessed: 14 January 2019).
Sassatelli, M. (2002) 'Imagined Europe: The shaping of a European cultural identity through EU cultural policy', *European Journal of Social Theory*, 5(4), pp. 435–451.
Sidorkin, A. (2002) 'Lyotard and Bakhtin: Engaged diversity in education', *Interchange*, 33(1), pp. 85–97.
Simon, R. I. (2012) 'Remembering together: Social media and the formation of the historical present', in Giaccardi, E. (ed.), *Heritage and social media*. London: Routledge, pp. 89–106.
Simone, V. (2009) 'Turin's museums as places for intercultural dialogue', in Bodo, S., Gibbs, K. and Sani, M. (eds.), *Museums as places for intercultural dialogue: Selected practices from Europe*. MAP for ID Group, pp. 32–47. Available at: www.ne-mo.org/fileadmin/Dateien/public/service/Handbook_MAPforID_EN.pdf (Accessed: 14 January 2019).
Smith, L. (2006) *Uses of heritage*. New York: Routledge.
Smith, L. and Waterton, E. (2010) 'The recognition and misrecognition of community heritage', *International Journal of Heritage Studies*, 16(1), pp. 4–15.
Srinivasan, R., Becvar, K. M., Boast, R. and Enote, J. (2010) 'Diverse knowledges and contact zones within the digital museum', *Science, Technology, & Human Values*, 35(5), pp. 735–768.
Stewart, J., Zediker, K. and Black, L. (2004) 'Relationships among philosophies of dialogue', in Anderson, R., Baxter, L. and Cissna, K. (eds.), *Dialogue: Theorizing difference in communication studies*. London: Sage Publications, pp. 21–38.
Sunstein, C. (2004) 'Democracy and filtering', *Communications of the ACM*, 47(12), pp. 57–59.
Taylor, J. and Gibson, L. K. (2017) 'Digitisation, digital interaction and social media: Embedded barriers to democratic heritage', *International Journal of Heritage Studies*, 23(5), pp. 408–420.
Tchen, J. K. W. (1992) 'Creating a dialogic museum: The Chinatown history museum experiment', in Karp, I., Kreamer, C. M. and Lavine, S. D. (eds.), *Museums and communities: The politics of public culture*. Washington, DC: Smithsonian Institution Press, pp. 285–326.
Thornton, M. (2007) 'Think outside the square you live in: Issues of difference and nation in virtual heritage', *Proceedings of the 13th intl conference on Virtual Systems and Multimedia (VSMM)*. Brisbane, Australia, 23–26 September, pp. 302–311.
Toplak, C. and Sumi, I. (2012) 'Europe(an union): Imagined community in the making?', *Journal of Contemporary European Studies*, 20(1), pp. 7–28.

UNESCO. (2015) *Recommendation concerning the protection and promotion of museums and collections, their diversity and their role in society*. Available at: http://unesdoc.unesco.org/images/0024/002463/246331m.pdf (Accessed: 14 January 2019).

UNESCO. (2017) *Survey on intercultural dialogue: Analysis of findings*. Available at: http://uis.unesco.org/sites/default/files/documents/unesco-survey-intercultural-dialogue-2017-analysis-findings-2018-en.pdf (Accessed: 14 January 2019).

UNESCO/UBC. (2012) *Vancouver declaration on the memory of the world in the digital age: Digitization and Preservation*. Available at: www.unesco.org/new/fileadmin/MULTIMEDIA/HQ/CI/CI/pdf/mow/unesco_ubc_vancouver_declaration_en.pdf (Accessed: 14 January 2019).

van den Akker, C. and Legêne, S. (2016) *Museums in a digital culture, how art and heritage become meaningful*. Amsterdam: Amsterdam University Press.

van Dijk, J. A. G. M. (2006) *The network society: Social aspects of new media*. 2nd edn. London: Sage.

Wegerif, R. (2008) 'Dialogic or dialectic? The significance of ontological assumptions in research on educational dialogue', *British Educational Research Journal*, 34(3), pp. 347–361.

Young, I. M. (1997) 'Asymmetrical reciprocity: On moral respect, wonder and enlarged thought', *Constellations*, 3(1), pp. 340–363.

3 Digitally enhanced polyvocality and reflective spaces

Challenges in sustaining dialogue in museums through digital technologies

Gabi Arrigoni and Areti Galani

Introduction

The idea of the exhibition as a form of metaphorical dialogue has been part of the discussion about the changing role of museums in past decades. In late 1990s, McLean (1999) pointed out how it was no longer clear who was talking and who was listening, as exhibitions were increasingly incorporating multiple voices and opportunities for expression and reflection. As some museums strive to become more socially accountable and to respond proactively to the concerns of modern society, the idea of the museum as a forum and a public sphere (Cameron, 1971; Ashley, 2005; Barrett, 2012) has progressively gained currency. This is particularly true for institutions of memory dealing with marginalised identities, difficult histories, migration or processes of democratisation. In this context, the term 'dialogue' has become part of a conventional institutional vocabulary used to describe the museum's role as site of understanding of different cultures and historical contingencies. Unsurprisingly, the idea of dialogue often features in museum programmes in the format of both displays and public events.

Furthermore, since the 1980s, digital technologies have been used in museums to reinvent interpretation, to enable the creation of content by visitors, support the coexistence of multiple perspectives and contribute to new forms of storytelling (Wyman *et al.*, 2011; Kidd, 2012; Pujol *et al.*, 2012). By experimenting with online platforms and social media, some museums have also expanded their activities outside their institutional boundaries. This digitally supported drive towards increasing access, visitor-centredness and openness of narratives poses the question of what the role of digital technologies is in extending the opportunities for dialogue in relation to heritage issues. Yet it is still unclear whether museums are effectively exploring the potential of the digital to address the challenging task of sustaining dialogue within and outside their walls.

Dialogue as a communicative practice epitomises the shift from a dissemination model of communication (one-to-many) to a networked one (many-to-many) (Carpentier, 2011; Drotner and Schrøder, 2014). In museum practice, it is also a particular feature of a broader culture of participation (Simon, 2008; Jewitt, 2012; Ridge, 2014). Furthermore, heritage institutions offer their audiences the opportunity to engage with socio-cultural and historical issues by increasingly making cultural content available through digitisation initiatives. In this respect, they form part of an ever-expanding ecology of knowledge sources and contribute to the abundance of information afforded by digital technologies. This expansion of information, argues Floridi (2014), challenges individuals to be more accountable and morally responsible towards society. Does this profusion of historical and personal memory accounts also impact dialogue? Do we have a better dialogue as a result of being exposed to more content, more points of view and more debates, or not? Issues of trust are also directly imbricated in these questions. Does the museum's reputation as a trusted institution (Fromm, Rekdal and Golding, 2014; Skorton, 2017), as opposed to other providers of information, particularly online sources and platforms, make it an especially suitable site for dialogue?

This chapter investigates these issues specifically in the context of the European Union (EU), where dialogue is often mobilised – for example, by policy makers as discussed by Galani et al. in Chapter 2 of this volume – as a means to negotiating diverse narratives related to the notion of 'encountering the other'. The first of these narratives relates to the supranational character of the EU; in this context, the history of Europe, from its ancient origins to the present, is frequently framed as a history of cross-border mobility, migration and multiculturalism to promote a communitarian sense of belonging (Jensen and Richardson, 2004; Poehls, 2011). This affirms a transnational identity that incorporates all European countries and provides historical context for discussing the contemporary politics of integration aimed at accommodating the current influx of migrants and refugees. The second narrative centres on the shared memory of the Holocaust and the atrocities of the Second World War (Levy and Sznaider, 2002). The origins of the EU's communitarian project are commonly framed as a response to these dramatic historical events (Probst, 2003; De Jong, 2011). Consequently, Europeanisation is often associated with a set of values that are intended to guarantee the unrepeatability of war and genocide (Kaiser, Krankenhagen and Poehls, 2014, pp. 113–153). The third narrative supporting the articulation of the European sense of belonging is the idea of democracy. In relation to Europeanisation, democracy has many faces: the shared heritage of the ancient Greek and Roman republics as foundations to the Western civilisation, the opposition to all forms of totalitarianism, the defence of human rights and a form of participatory and accountable governance (Chryssochoou, 2000; Follesdal and Koslowski, 2013). These narratives, we argue, are leading some museums in Europe to develop dialogic displays, and opportunities for dialogue, as an integral part of their curatorial strategy. Against this background, the idea of promoting dialogue through museums can be understood as important in the European context *precisely* because it promises a means of achieving the democratic process, so central to the EU project.

Throughout this chapter, we exemplify how dialogic approaches in museums are mobilised to support these narratives through engagement with digital technologies. We intimate how digital technologies are suitable not just to materialise the coexistence of different voices, but also to evoke a sense of transience and flow that can effectively represent the idea of Europe as a project in constant becoming (Rigney, 2012, p. 608), providing a sense of agency to those who participate in this process. The chapter initially reviews key ideas connected to dialogue-driven museology. This is followed by an explication of the methodological approach that underpins this research. Subsequently, we discuss three dimensions of dialogue emerging from the fieldwork connected to the themes of (a) polyvocality, (b) civic listening and (c) the tension between institutional and online spaces for dialogue. The chapter concludes with a reflection on the barriers and opportunities for digitally mediated dialogue in museums that deal with the European narratives outlined earlier. We argue that the limited digital experimentation on digital dialogues is rooted in a perceived distance between technology-mediated and human dialogic capacities. Furthermore, we discuss the dialogic potential of digital technologies to enhance listening and opportunities for reflection in the exhibition space, and we reflect on the role of multimedia and multisensory environments in shaping identity construction and representation processes in museums.

Digital practices for a dialogue-driven museology

The idea of a dialogue-driven museology was initially developed in relation to exhibiting history (Tchen, 1992) to support new forms of reciprocity between institutions and communities with a stake in the museum's activities (see also Clifford, 1997). A core objective of these dialogic practices was the re-balancing of power inequality between audiences and institutions resulting from long-established collecting and exhibiting practices connected to colonial ideals. In this context, dialogue was conceptualised as a collective, reciprocal thinking process, intended as a way of leading to deeper understandings of the other. It did not, however, necessarily lead to institutional change. Therefore, subsequent scholarly work criticised these initial attempts on dialogic museum practice as forms of appropriation and normalisation, which lacked awareness of issues of oppositionality and maintained the dominant role of the institution (Bennett, 1998, p. 213; Boast, 2011; Harris, 2011). Responding to this critique, subsequent re-examinations of the notion of the 'dialogic museum' put an emphasis on alternative forms of reflexive museology intended as a process of institutional transformation, which would enable institutions to be more responsive and able to listen to and to answer back to society (Harris, 2011; Hernández Hernández, 2011; Brulon Soares, 2011). In these texts, museums are considered dialogic not for their capacity to host dialogue-based events with their communities, but primarily because they are situated at the intersection of cultures, individuals and experience.

Furthermore, with the advance of digital technologies, cultural institutions have identified an opportunity to experiment with museum experiences co-curated and co-created with their communities by increasingly appropriating techniques from the field of design. There is a natural affinity between the objectives of the two fields as design practices, particularly those from the traditions of participatory design (Schuler and Namioka, 1993) and co-design (Sanders and Stappers, 2008), see the process of designing technologies as a collective inquiry into people's concerns and attitudes. Stuedahl *et al.* in this volume (Chapter 4) provide a focused exploration of this kind of practice. For example, the exhibition *Digital Natives* at the Aarhus Centre for Contemporary Art (Iversen and Smith, 2012) took full advantage of the potential of participatory design practices to explore young people's everyday communication practices within the museum's space. In this project, participants were perceived not as mere informants but were engaged in 'a process of dialogic curation based on mutual engagement, trust and reciprocity' (ibid., p. 111) leading to the co-production of the exhibition installations. Smørdal, Stuedahl and Sem (2014) suggest that the interweaving of social media and museological practices in the co-design of museum displays creates what they call 'experimental zones'. Within the frame of experimental zones, museums as dialogic institutions can support co-curation initiatives that aim to create and support multidirectional communication opportunities involving museum staff and audiences across both analogue and digital platforms.

While the *Digital Natives* exhibition exemplifies a specific dialogic approach to museum co-curation approaches through design, the most prominent application of digital technologies to support dialogue in exhibition spaces is through the incorporation of personal accounts and testimonies of ordinary people in the displays. Digital tools support the storage and retrieval of multimedia content and allow the presentation of oral history archives to the public through interactive and accessible interfaces. Additionally, they make possible the inclusion of contributions generated by

Enhanced polyvocality and reflective spaces 41

visitors during their visit, materialising, to some extent, the theorisations of the museum as participatory media and an embodiment of the public sphere (Noy, 2016). Several museums, for instance, have developed digital stations for visitors to record audio-visual messages that can subsequently be browsed, listened to and answered to in an asynchronous fashion. This strategy crafts possibilities of indirect and asynchronous encounters between visitors as well as the awareness that one's own voice can be discovered by others (National Museum of American Jewish History, n.d.; Henry, 2015). Through these practices, digital media have the capacity to enhance polyvocality while enabling what Witcomb (2003) calls a dialogic approach to interactivity (p. 163); Witcomb further argues that multimedia displays are 'suited to a notion of history as a set of fragments', encouraging more inquisitive attitudes in the visitor (ibid., p. 161). This suggests that digital technologies in the museum space have the potential to break down monologic narratives and help visitors to more easily perceive the coexistence of multiple, parallel and, often, conflictual, meanings. This can also increase the visitors' perception that their perspectives cannot be expressed only within but also can shape the museum space.

Recent technological advances have also instigated more literal incorporations of digitally mediated dialogues in exhibition spaces – a topic that we revisit later in this chapter. In these cases, digital tools are used to orchestrate question-and-answer–based interactions between visitors and museum staff or between visitors and digitally generated characters. For instance, the *ASK* mobile app developed by the Brooklyn Museum in 2016 offers visitors the opportunity to ask direct questions about the displays to the 'experts' behind the scenes and receive responses during their visit. Similar dynamics can be found in a fast-emerging body of applications deploying chat-bots, often adopted as an alternative way of providing interpretative content (Boiano, Cuomo and Gaia, 2016; Vassos *et al.*, 2016). Regardless of whether chat-bots respond to questions from the visitors or solicit visitors' responses with a set of prompts, the dialogic interaction happens between a visitor interlocutor and a digital interface retrieving pre-packaged sentences from a database or synthesising new language on a keyword basis. This raises questions around the definition of a digitally mediated dialogic experience: can dialogue still take place if one of the interlocutors is a non-human actor? Although one might argue that the automated and predetermined nature of many digital museum installations is frequently perceived as antithetical to dialogue, the *liveness* of these technologies has the capacity to prompt the same reflective, emotional and critical response to the visitor as dialogue with another human being.

This selective summary of digitally enabled dialogic practices indicates that digital technologies for dialogue tend to be used by museums as part of their institutional participatory and experiential strategies. In some cases, digital technologies are combined with design approaches to support co-curation practices and decision-making processes in the development of exhibits and displays. Dialogic digital interactions are facilitated through apps, self-contained installations and articulated multimedia environments where dialogue operates as a dynamic form of engagement and an instrument for museum interpretation. To understand the challenges and opportunities of extending digitally enabled dialogue within exhibition spaces beyond this participatory framework, the study presented in this chapter focuses on how digital technologies support dialogue in museums that address difficult and often contested European narratives; this context, we argue, allows us to formulate a more civic and politically oriented conceptualisation of digitally mediated dialogue in the exhibition floor.

Methodology

This chapter draws on fieldwork that examined the role of digital technologies in supporting dialogic practices in a small selection of European museums that address notions of otherness in historical, social and identitarian narratives in Europe. The fieldwork involved interviews with museum professionals and display analysis of exhibitions in ten museums during 2017–2018. In particular, the study involves the Galata, Museum of the Sea, in Genoa (specifically the *Memory and Migration* display); the Mudec, Museum of Cultures, in Milan; the Museum of European Cultures (MEK) in Berlin; and the recent Museum for Intercultural Dialogue (MID) in Kielce, all of which deal with cross-border mobility, interculturality and migration in Europe, with a focus on Italy, Germany and Poland, respectively. We also visited the National Holocaust Centre and Museum (NHCM) in Laxton, UK; the POLIN Museum of the History of Polish Jews in Warsaw; and the Jewish Museum Berlin (JMB), all of which address the Central European narrative of the Holocaust and the history of Jewish people in Europe. The study also involves the European Solidarity Centre in Gdansk, Poland (ECS); the People's History Museum (PHM) in Manchester, UK; and the National Museums Liverpool, UK, all three of which address processes of democratisation and civic participation within European countries. These institutions were selected to be included in the study because they shared one or more of the following characteristics: (a) a focus on histories related to the process of Europeanisation or a particular emphasis on issues of identity and place-making in European context, and (b) the use of the term 'dialogue' in their mission statement or other public forms of self-representations, such as in the 'About' section on their website.

Enhanced polyvocality and reflective spaces 43

We conducted ten in-depth semi-structured interviews with senior managers affiliated to the curatorial, scientific and digital publishing departments of these museums[1] – we iteratively introduce our interviewees as we draw on our conversations with them in the following sections of this chapter. The interviews involved a set of questions common to all interviewees, for example, their definition of dialogue and how their institutions use digital tools to sustain heritage-related dialogues; they also included questions specifically tailored to each context. Alongside the interviews, display analysis fieldnotes were collected from the sites. We used thematic analysis to develop insights from the collected materials. The analysis pointed towards specific institutional narratives, functions and visions connected to the ideas of polyvocality, civic listening and an expanded on-site/online dialogic space, which we discuss in turn in the following sections.

Digitally enhanced polyvocality

The uncovering of marginalised narratives and the deconstruction of knowledge generation processes is at the heart of the dialogic museum's aspiration to reimagine how museums engage with social and public history. Drawing on the fieldwork, this section discusses how museums use digital exhibits to represent the public's involvement in the construction of history and collective memory (see also Mason, Whitehead and Graham, 2013) and to encourage visitors' responses. Whilst polyvocality resonates with the democratic subtext of the European project (Kohler-Koch, 2012), we also observed that the majority of the digital exhibits we looked at, which focused on providing access to the memories of ordinary people, were consistently framed in relation to a local or a global scale rather than a European one. Furthermore, the dialogic interactions put forward by these exhibits often presented the story of the 'other' as both distinct and often disconnected from a more consciously articulated transnational narrative of the respective region or country.

A common theme in the discussion with our interviewees concerned an institutional commitment to promote multiple perspectives and voices. For example, Joanna Fikus, head of exhibitions at POLIN, which resolutely focuses on the presentation of the history of Polish Jews, clearly indicated that 'multiperspectivity' is very important to showcase not only variety but also difference among perspectives included in an exhibition: 'we are showing different voices, from the period, but very different'. This makes particular sense in POLIN, because it aims to highlight that Jewish history occupies a broader chronological span that goes beyond the Holocaust. Others, such as Gianni Carosio, curator at Galata, and Joanna Król, head of digital collections at POLIN, highlighted the role of digital technologies in terms of recording, archiving and making available a large number of contributions from ordinary people. Several digital displays in these institutions provided access to multiple personal stories, in the form of archive-like exhibits, multimedia environments and participatory interpretative tools. The displays in the Museum of Intercultural Dialogue (MID) in Kielce epitomise the archival format; its digital oral history archive contains recordings of inhabitants of the Świętokrzyskie province sharing experiences of the Second World War. According to the archivist at the time of the interview, these materials have value 'because they are based on truth' and will be made accessible to the public to deliver the 'emotions' of these histories. It appears, therefore, that the museum staff in MID see in the first-hand nature of this material an opportunity to support an encounter between the visitors and the witnesses of the local past that is free from other interventions. Furthermore, digital interfaces have been used in the majority of the museums we visited (ECS, Galata, PHM, JMB, POLIN, MID, MEK) to enable visitors to choose from a plethora of oral history resources incorporated in the exhibitions.

While it is rare to find exhibits allowing visitors to directly formulate a question or initiate a dialogic interaction, several installations exploit interactivity to allow the selection of particular questions or contributions, thus recreating, in part, the feeling of having a conversation. At POLIN, one of the interactive video installations presents different accounts on contemporary Jewish life in Poland. The public can select to listen to one or more questions, answered by one of 25 potential respondents. The curatorial challenge in this room is to introduce the nature of contemporary history as not yet written and open ended; this is addressed here by using a bare, minimal white space. Within this unembellished space, the interactive videos engender a sense of a direct encounter between visitors and Jewish individuals, providing insights into contemporary Jewish life and experiences in Poland.

Polyvocality is taken to an environmental dimension at the Galata, where the last section of the permanent exhibition *Memory and Migration* describes the transition of Italy from a country of migrants to one of immigration and addresses contemporary tensions by emphasising the benefits of a multicultural society (Figure 3.1).

This space adopts a graphic, minimalistic style with significant use of infographics – a common approach in exhibitions about migration (e.g. Little and Watson, 2015), including a timeline of immigration to Italy from 1973 to the present. Several multimedia displays in the exhibition counteract this emphasis on data by giving expression to individual stories of immigration. For instance, a set of audio-visual interactives allows visitors to select and listen to the stories of African immigrants now living in Genoa.

Figure 3.1 Memory and Migration, contemporary section, at Galata Museo del Mare.
Source: Photo: Gabi Arrigoni.

These are a small portion of a broader digital archive entirely accessible on the YouTube channel *Archive of the Migrant Memory*, an ongoing project initiated by Galata in 2015 (Galata Museo del Mare, 2018). Another exhibit shows an animation in which a cartoon-like character, in the style of didactic and promotional videos, introduces himself and, while addressing the viewers, advocates the positive aspects of immigration by providing statistics and factual information. Pseudo-dialogic features such as addressing the listener or telling one's own story are adopted to both deliver information and generate empathy and emotional engagement. Dialogue in this exhibition is embedded within a space characterised by multimodal and layered ways of delivering information and different styles of visitor experience, evoking the interweaving of histories and cultural influences shaping European identities.

Finally, some institutions implement polyvocality as part of the interpretation they provide for the individual museum objects in their exhibition. For instance, Mudec, the Museum of Cultures in Milan that holds a collection mostly constituted by artefacts from cultures outside Europe, has solicited the perspective of second-generation immigrants living in Milan to discuss artefacts and works of art associated with their country of origin, included in the permanent exhibition. Selected objects are explained by 'didascalie partecipate' (participatory labels) accessible through a QR code. As Giorgia Barzetti, conservator in Mudec, explained, these labels are the product of workshops in which children from migrant communities developed their own subjective interpretation of the objects in response to a guided visit to the exhibition.

The aforementioned examples illustrate how dialogue in museums can be identified as a feature of interpretative and interactive approaches oriented towards giving visibility to multiple points of view and orchestrating a perception of the museum as capable of letting go of its monologic voice (Adair, Filene and Koloski, 2011). The availability of a variety of testimonies and contributions by ordinary people is a feature that would not be easily achieved in a display without digital technologies and is pivotal in suggesting that no particular voices are prioritised over others. In the context of the European museums in the study, what we define as digitally enhanced polyvocality is associated with the topic of migration and cross-cultural encounters in mediating and representing the process of getting to know 'the other'. However, while the dialogic mechanisms in place have the capacity to promote respect for difference and counter notions of racism by humanising 'the other', they show little interest in commenting on ideas and ideals of transnationalism that characterise the European project. As a matter of fact, we are not proposing an intrinsically positive judgement on transnationalism as opposed to national or local perspectives; neither have we advocated that European museums should promote transnationalism because of their country's membership in the European Union (EU). However, in analysing dialogue within the context of European museums and the relevant policies, as discussed by Galani et al. in Chapter 2 of this volume, it is inevitable to consider how the EU vision is expressed within its heritage institutions. Despite the European dimension of the narratives at stake, the polyvocal displays appear to be focused on the regional or national perspective: Jews in Poland, migrants arriving to Genoa, migrant communities in Milan or memories of the local province. The dialogic structure itself, in a way, contributes to a clear separation between locals or museum visitors, cast in the role of listeners, and the newcomers telling their stories.

Beyond these limitations, however, European values can find poetic expression in digitally enhanced environments, featuring sensorial, emotional and informational inputs that set the scene for dialogue, best exemplified by Galata. The richness of content and the flow of voices and memories function as representations of a potential, ongoing conversation about what a transcultural and transnational identity could be. Dialogic approaches in

Enhanced polyvocality and reflective spaces 47

this respect can be identified not so much in reference to isolated exhibits and interactions, but as an underlying characteristic of the exhibition space as a whole. As such, these spaces embody a notion of Europeanisation as an evolving process in need of constant renegotiation and require the visitor to approach them with a sense of openness, which is also a condition for dialogic encounters.

Dialogic listening and civic reflexivity

As shown earlier, most digitally enabled dialogic interactions in museums are based on asymmetric relationships between speakers and listeners, frequently casting visitors in the listening role. This section correlates understandings of dialogue emerged from the interviews with an exploration of the value of listening as an active component of the dialogic process, crucial for the transformative, educational and civic aims of many heritage organisations. It demonstrates that digital technologies can most effectively express their dialogic potential by providing opportunities for visitors to engage in personal inquiry and self-questioning.

When asked about their own definitions of dialogue, interviewees frequently provided a set of key requisites, among which *openness* featured prominently, as a form of intellectual honesty and refusal of prejudice and preconceived truths. Jacek Kołtan, deputy director of the European Solidarity Centre (ESC) in Gdansk, associated dialogue with the challenges of understanding difference. Indeed, ECS aims to address the history of the Solidarity movement in Poland within a broader perspective of democratic opposition 'to share the achievements of a peaceful struggle for freedom, justice, democracy and human rights with those who are deprived of them' ('The Mission', ECS website). Several interviewees connected *openness* to difference to notions of listening and attentiveness towards 'the other' as Joanna Fikus at POLIN clearly states: '[dialogue is] when you are open and when you listen. It's a very simple answer'. This sense of being open to listening to the other person's story allows visitors, according to Louise Stafford, education officer at the National Holocaust Centre and Museum (NHCM), to 'consider the impact of individuals within their story and gives the chance to see the complexity of that and the importance of that'.

The *Forever Project*, currently in ongoing development in the NHCM, best epitomises the experience of digitally mediated listening within the museum. The piece used 3D film technology to simulate a live encounter with a Holocaust survivor, anticipating a future when Holocaust survivors will no longer be able to share their story. Different from a traditional video-recording, it enables visitors not only to listen to the story but also to ask questions to the 'virtual' survivor, and to receive an answer. The latter is facilitated by a piece of software that queries over a thousand pre-recorded answers in the system's database. This means that questions outside the coverage of the recordings are skipped or replaced by pre-anticipated questions by the installation's facilitator. The system allows for a realistic and immersive simulation of dialogue, with the opportunity to feel closer to the (absent) survivor. While this is one of the most literal examples of digitally enabled dialogues in our study, the roles of the visitor and that of the survivor are profoundly asymmetric. Although visitors are offered the chance to ask a question, their role broadly remains that of a listener, and priority is given to what the survivor says.

Admittedly, several of our interviewees conceptualised the dialogic intentions of their exhibits as achieving more than listening to personal stories. One of the key outcomes of listening for them was the capacity of exhibits to encourage visitors to engage with contemporary issues. For example, Phil Lyons, CEO at NHCM, clearly pointed to the role of certain exhibits to highlight the significance of the past in the present (Smith, Wetherell and Campbell, 2018) in order to inspire visitors to reflect on current sociopolitical debates:

> I want young people particularly to go away from here thinking not just how dreadful that was, but what caused it, what's happening today, what does it mean for me, what responsibility I've got to preventing a similar thing happening today.

Similarly, Gianni Carosio connected Galata's dialogic mission to the intention to engage visitors with the complexity of historical and contemporary issues by stimulating questions in visitors, often in relation to their own preconceptions:

> There is the desire to show our visitors that we are facing very complex times and that nobody has a clear idea of how to deal with it. Messages need to be open, stimulate questions in the visitor, break his *[sic]* own certainties, which is sometimes uncomfortable. But this is life. If somebody leaves Galata with questions we have achieved our aim.

The intention of these museum professionals to mobilise listening within the museum towards a more active participation in current cultural and political life aligns with Annette's (2009) notion of 'civic listening'. Annette, writing on citizenship, suggests 'civic listening' as a necessary skill that should be the foundation of participatory democracy. Distinct and complementary to 'civic speaking', civic listening 'would include both levels of emotional literacy and intercultural understanding' (ibid., p. 157), supporting citizens in recognising differences and enabling a shared political identity (ibid., p. 156).

Within the museum space, creating spaces for civic listening and reflection might require some rudimentary intervention in terms of exhibition design, such as the provision of tables and chairs, alongside more tailored scenographic interventions and installations towards the creation of immersive and intimate spaces. Multimedia, experiential environments and particular spatial arrangement can support the preliminary conditions for dialogue by providing time and space for visitors to explore individual standpoints and question their assumptions. The MID metaphorically reconstructs this process through a three-room articulation in their exhibition space that evidences how multimedia are pivotal in materialising flow and openness. In this arrangement, the first room displays successful examples of multiculturalism from Poland, while the second room is conceived as a labyrinth, to represent the difficulties encountered when one deals with different cultures. This leads to the third room, called *The Diversity Triangle* (see Figure 3.2),

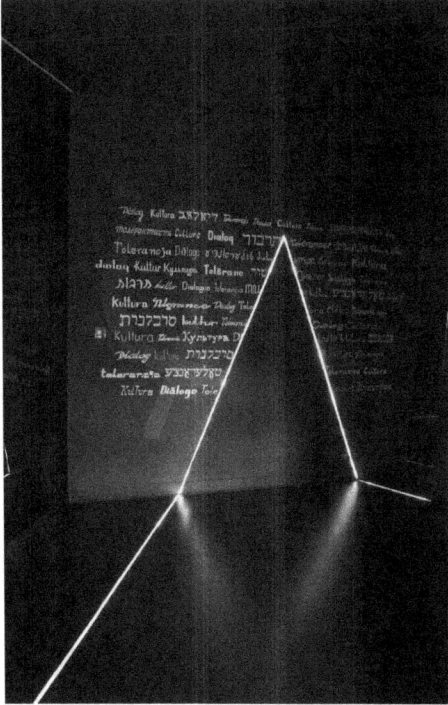

Figure 3.2 The Diversity Triangle at Museum for Intercultural Dialogue.
Source: Photo: Wojciech Cedro.

where multimedia technologies enable the visitors to access, negotiate and reflect on a range of resources on topics such as the Rwandan Genocide, Roma culture and Polish Armenians. Here, multimedia content is essential to the *liveness* and *immersion* of the experience as a means to increasing the audience's attentiveness to 'the other'. In the words of the archivist in MID, 'you do something very good, you try to communicate with someone'.

A more focused approach is observed at the Jewish Museum Berlin (JMB), where a room is dedicated to the pre–First World War debates around Jewish emancipation and the rights of Jewish people in Germany. Here, an interactive table with phone-like handsets (see Figure 3.3) allows visitors to listen to a range of historical media, mostly comprising political speeches.

By selecting questions such as 'Should Jews be granted the same rights as Christians?' or 'Can a Jew be a German?' visitors are exposed to the original arguments as presented in public debates by commentators of the past, instead of receiving a pre-digested summary through the institutional interpretative voice. With disembodied voices from official speeches, this display is not about encountering otherness, but rather about reflecting on different points of view and questioning one's own personal stance in the face of historical sources.

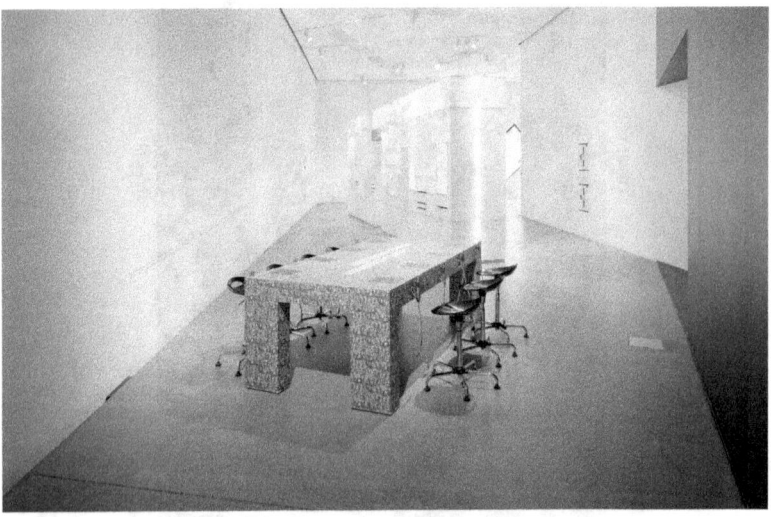

Figure 3.3 The emancipation of the Jews – historical debates *1801–1912* at the Jewish Museum Berlin.

Source: Picture credits: Jewish Museum Berlin, Photo: Volker Kreidler, Berlin.

Despite the potential of digital technologies in advancing active and civic forms of listening in the selection of examples outlined earlier, the link between the creation of digitally mediated reflective environments and the explicit promotion of dialogue in the museum space was never explicitly advanced by our interviewees. We argue that this was often rooted in a particular, non-digital conceptualisation of dialogue held by many of our interviewees, which we discuss in the following section.

Keeping it under control: digital vs. institutional spaces for heritage dialogue

Our analysis of the interviews suggests that, overall, the idea of digitally enabled dialogue has received limited attention by exhibition curators and designers in the European institutions in our fieldwork. Besides practical challenges associated with the implementation of digital technologies in museums, the interviews show that specific understandings of dialogue as a deeply human process, held by museum professionals, discourage the use of digital tools for this purpose. Several of the interviewees, Gianni Carosio at Galata; Barbara Thiele, head of digital at JMB; and Joanna Król at POLIN, shared the perception of dialogue as something that takes place face-to-face 'between people' as a two-way process allowing a circular dynamic of responses:

> I believe that dialogue is between two people so I think that real dialogue is definitely happening during our educational activities and cultural activities when you can face different people and this is very direct, this is what I believe. And as for all of the things we have here, including websites, different exhibitions, core exhibition, I believe this is more about giving an opportunity to audience to reflect on history, memory.
>
> (Joanna Król, POLIN)

This character of direct, human exchange was emphasised as antithetical to the idea of digitally mediated dialogue, in which digital technology is deemed incapable of effectively addressing the dialogic needs of the public. For instance, Gianni Carosio contends, 'I am convinced that dialogue is something that takes place between people. It is not even fair to invest the multimedia of objectives that it will never be able to achieve'.

Conversely, Hogsden and Poulter (2012), researching the role of online institutional portals in supporting institutional collecting practices of ethnographic material alongside source communities, advance the concept of a 'digital contact zone' to suggest the potential of digital platforms to support dialogue about heritage outside the actual institutional perimeters. Whilst the museum is a space of inequality and asymmetrical power, they argue, the online realm might allow more ambiguous and open articulations, unfettered by institutional interpretative frameworks. Our interviewees also talked about the attempts of their institutions to expand their role as public spheres online, but they also specifically reflected on the challenges they faced in deciding how to deal with potentially inappropriate online behaviours.

Social media, in particular, generate complex ethical challenges for museums that need to consider risks associated with the sensitive nature of their content while attempting to establish a deeper conversation with their audiences. Discussing the case of the United States Holocaust Memorial Museum, Wong (2011) explores how engaging with social media recasts and exacerbates traditional 'questions raised about transparency, censorship, respect for constituencies' (p. 102). The immediacy and public dimension of comments on platforms such as YouTube, Twitter or Facebook impose difficult choices for museums in terms of moderating users' contributions. Especially in the case of the Jewish genocide, social media may offer an unintentional stage for anti-Semitic attacks and disrespectful comments. Institutions in these cases tend to prioritise their memorial function and the respect for victims and survivors over issues of free speech, transparency and openness (ibid. 2011, p. 105). In the interviews, this concern was voiced several times, indicating a common approach towards limiting or discouraging online comments. The following reflection by Joanna Król, head of digital collections at POLIN, in relation to her team's approach to social media, is highly indicative:

> I think in the last few weeks in my department with my colleagues we came to the conclusion that in fact first of all we don't know if we really still relate to real dialogue and another issue is that we are very passive and we are not exactly open for this dialogue, and you can even see that in the way we post things, we don't provoke people to comment because we had so many nasty unpleasant anti-Semitic comments that we don't want to go *[sic]* into conversation with these anti-Semitic people. So we are more passive, we don't exactly ask our visitors to be active and this is a paradox because in theory we would expect that thanks to these tools we could communicate with people but this is not in fact the thing we want to do.

Hence, the creation of bespoke web platforms is a preferred choice when museums seek to involve online communities. For instance, *Jewish Places* (Jewish Museum Berlin, 2018) is a participatory database bringing together

Enhanced polyvocality and reflective spaces 53

local information of sites relevant to Jewish life, previously found in independent blogs and archives. The museum acts as a point of convergence for disseminated, disconnected content, with the possibility for everyone to contribute or correct the data. POLIN has also developed websites documenting aspects of Jewish life through personal testimonies, photographs and archival material. *The Polish Righteous* (POLIN, 2016) gathers stories of Polish people who helped Jews during the Holocaust; the *Virtual Shtetl* (POLIN, 2017) documents the presence of Jewish heritage in Polish towns. One of the reasons the Internet is regarded as a useful space for heritage content by the interviewees is its capacity to 'to keep equal rights to everyone else, every Jewish person, doesn't matter from which country, to have equal rights to learn about their heritage' (Joanna Król, POLIN). Nevertheless, the dialogic potential of these platforms does not feature as a priority in the case study museums; rather, they use them as an opportunity for broader circulation of content. So, while in the eyes of our interviewees Dana Muller, researcher on the *Jewish Places* project, and Joanna Król, these platforms are hardly perceived as dialogic, they are relevant insofar they expand the circulation of knowledge around the histories and heritages at stake, proliferating opportunities for the kind of transcultural encounter that is at the core of the museums' dialogic missions and key to the European project.

Opportunities and challenges for digitally enhanced heritage dialogues

The cases examined exemplify representations of otherness and articulations of subjectivity in which 'the other' is a counterpart in dialogue. De Jong (2011) argues that the use of video testimonies in exhibitions dealing with European identity is pivotal to constructing a sense of shared history and modelling the European citizen. These affirmations of common history and values, however, collide with a rather undefined idea of Europe, whose main feature is to be an ongoing process of incorporation of national and regional entities (Krankenhagen, 2011). However, as digital dialogic exhibits tend to maintain a clear distinction between speaker and listener, their capacity to specifically engage with complex, transcultural and transnational perspectives on identity is limited. As a result, one is left with the impression of cultures and individuals facing each other, potentially able to achieve mutual understanding but far from negotiating forms of mixed identities or new and transformed 'imagined communities' (Anderson, 1983). The regional, local point of view appears as the primary lens to represent the encounter with the other, while the composite dimension of Europe as a transnational, or at least supranational, process does not emerge in these displays. Despite the potential of the digital to cross borders, it is its repository nature that is mostly used by institutions, thus reinforcing the idea of Europe as an aggregate of multiple localities that do not suggest any feeling of being implicated in each other's culture.

Questions of institutional space and its inherent limitations in terms of encouraging conflict (Bennett, 2005; Lynch, 2014) are pivotal in this discussion and reinforce a general resistance to designing for dialogue in the core exhibition space. Hence, opportunities for dialogue are most commonly provided within educational programmes, as it was testified by many of our interviewees, which usually carries a hierarchical and predefined division of roles between facilitators and participants. However, the multisensoriality and multimodality of digital media allow visitors to encounter heterogeneous and layered environments delivering a sense of suspension and complexity that have the potential to stimulate processes of inquiry. The key digital features of archivability, multimodality and asynchronicity, which underpin the polyvocal and reflective character of many displays, serve the representation of Europe as an evolving entity engaged in a particularly transformative process. The richness of information and the dynamic flow of voices, stories and messages have the potential to deliver a sense of openness, uncertainty, suspension of judgement and transformation. Whereas polyvocality in itself does not constitute dialogue, it generates a diffused awareness that what is being said in museums can be questioned and contested, and that different truths may simultaneously coexist.

Going back to the key European narratives discussed earlier in this chapter, this sense of openness and uncertainty support the idea of a multiplicity of identities (interculturality), in which the encounter with the other is necessary and enriching (acceptance of difference) and in which everyone has the right and duty to have an informed opinion and to be listened to (democratic principle). Further, the emphasis on personal accounts helps to frame cultural difference as a difference of life experience, which can better respond to European appraisals of identity as a composite entity in which one is both foreign and domestic (Rigney, 2012, p. 609). We also infer from the analysis of the displays that digital media can potentially support certain preliminary conditions of dialogue such as awareness of the other and the other's feelings. Digital resources may generate temporary coming together among visitors, around the dissemination of a shared piece of knowledge or a conversational prompt, which can inspire our capacity to recognise different perspectives. In saying this, we are mindful of Witcomb's (2015) 'pedagogy of feeling,' which suggests a move forward, beyond the mere inclusion of different voices in the museum, and towards recognising the role of sensorial and affective exhibition strategies in supporting new forms of cross-cultural encounters characterised by reciprocity and mutual responsibility.

Enhanced polyvocality and reflective spaces 55

While digital tools as currently used do not seem to be suitable for facilitating extended dialogues within exhibition spaces, they can support the articulation of fragments, snapshots of dialogue, such as questions, answers and opinions that can contribute to broader asynchronous collective dialogues. Digital dialogues might be fragmentary; therefore, thinking about how to scaffold a dialogic experience through digital means could be a fruitful approach in beginning such a design process. Engaging more consciously in design experimentation around the aforementioned digital features, as discussed by Stuedahl *et al.* in Chapter 4 of this volume, presents a way forward to disentangling heritage dialogues from traditional mechanisms of intercultural juxtaposition towards emphasising, instead, opportunities for reflection and for the recognition of fluid and mutable processes of identity construction. Ultimately, to address this issue, one should consider the upstream argument of the role of digital technologies in shifting the perceptions around the mission of the museum itself and its transition from knowledge gatekeeper to site of experience, co-production and social interaction.

What emerges from our investigation is the irreducible tension between different institutional scales. As discussed in Chapter 2 in this volume, at the macro-institutional scale that links to policy discourse, dialogue is framed in very abstract terms as a tool to encourage social cohesion and multiculturalism. By contrast, when institutions translate their visions and missions into actions, initiatives and displays, dialogue tends to be reshaped through storytelling, interpretative and participatory techniques. In this context, dialogue remains an end in itself, with little potency in encouraging visitors to become active citizens as a result of their museum experience. This gap is the result of a complex ecology that cuts across different scales of governance and in which the relationship between individuals, institutions and their respective agencies requires further investigation. It is clear, however, that although digital technologies are not purposefully used to reimagine the dialogic potential of these institutions, they generate immersive, rich in content, dynamic, and intimate environments that influence dialogic practices in a variety of ways, most of which require further and urgent attention within the museum space and the museological discourse.

Acknowledgements

We would like to thank all the interviewees for generously contributing their time to have discussions with us about their practices and to facilitate our visits in their exhibitions. This chapter would not be possible without them. We would also like to thank our colleague Dr Susannah Eckersley, for contributing to the collection of materials for this research, and our colleague Dr Joanne Sayner, who provided feedback on early versions of this chapter. This research was carried out as part of the CoHERE (2016–2019) project, which has received funding from the European Union Horizon 2020 programme under grant agreement NO 693289.

Note

1 All affiliations reflect people's roles at the time of the interviews 2017–2018.

References

Adair, B., Filene, B. and Koloski, L. (2011) *Letting go?: Sharing historical authority in a user-generated world*. Walnut Creek: Left Coast Press.

Anderson, B. (1983) *Imagined communities: Reflections on the origin and spread of nationalism*. London: Verso.

Annette, J. (2009) '"Active learning for active citizenship": Democratic citizenship and lifelong learning', *Education, Citizenship and Social Justice*, 4(2), pp. 149–160.

Ashley, S. (2005) 'State authority and the public sphere: Ideas on the changing role of the museum as a Canadian social institution', *Museum and Society*, 3(1), pp. 5–17.

Barrett, J. (2012) *Museums and the public sphere*. Chichester: John Wiley & Sons.

Bennett, T. (1998) *Culture: A reformers' science*. London: Sage.

Bennett, T. (2005) 'Civic laboratories: Museums, cultural objecthood and the governance of the social', *Cultural Studies*, 19(5), pp. 521–547.

Boast, R. (2011) 'Neocolonial collaboration: Museum as contact zone revisited', *Museum Anthropology*, 34(1), pp. 56–70.

Boiano, S., Cuomo, P. and Gaia, G. (2016) 'Real-time messaging platforms for storytelling and gamification in museums: A case history in Milan', in *Proceedings of The Electronic Visulisation and the Arts (EVA 2016)*. London: Electronic Workshops in Computing (eWiC), pp. 291–293.

Brulon Soares, B. (2011) 'Experiencing dialogue: behind the curtains of museum performance', in *The Dialogic Museum and the visitor experience: ICOFOM Study Series, Issue 40*, pp. 33-42. Available at: http://network.icom.museum/fileadmin/user_upload/minisites/icofom/pdf/ISS%2040_ch_web2.pdf (Accessed: 7 January 2019).

Cameron, D. (1971) 'The museum, a temple or the forum', *Curator: The Museum Journal*, 14(1), pp. 11–24.

Carpentier, N. (2011) 'Contextualising audience-author convergences: "New" technologies' claims to increased participation, novelty and uniqueness', *Cultural Studies*, 25(4–5), pp. 517–533.

Chryssochoou, D. (2000) *Democracy in the European Union*. London: I.B. Tauris.

Clifford, J. (1997) *Routes: Travel and translation in the late twentieth century*. Cambridge, MA: Harvard University Press.

De Jong, S. (2011) 'Is this us? The construction of European woman/man in the exhibition it's our history!', *Culture Unbound: Journal of Current Cultural Research*, 3(3), pp. 369–383.

Enhanced polyvocality and reflective spaces 57

Drotner, K. and Schrøder, K. C. (2014) *Museum communication and social media: The connected museum*. New York and London: Routledge.
Floridi, L. (2014) *The fourth revolution: How the infosphere is reshaping human reality*. Oxford: Oxford University Press.
Follesdal, A. and Koslowski, P. (2013) *Democracy and the European Union*. Berlin: Springer.
Fromm, A., Rekdal, P. B. and Golding, V. (2014) *Museums and truth*. Newcastle upon Tyne: Cambridge Scholars Publishing.
Galata Museo del Mare. (2018) *Archive of the migrant memory, memory and migration*. Available at: www.memoriaemigrazioni.it/prt_page.asp?idSez=406 (Accessed: 3 December 2018).
Harris, J. (2011) 'Dialogism and the visitor experience', in *The Dialogic Museum and the visitor experience: ICOFOM Study Series, Issue 40*, pp. 9–10. Available at: http://network.icom.museum/fileadmin/user_upload/minisites/icofom/pdf/ISS%2040_ch_web2.pdf (Accessed: 7 January 2019).
Henry, D. (2015) 'Talking deeper about cultural difference: A digital interactive from Melbourne', *Curator: The Museum Journal*, 58(2), pp. 209–222.
Hernández Hernández, H. (2011) 'Dialogic museum and social communication', in *The Dialogic Museum and the visitor experience: ICOFOM Study Series, Issue 40*, pp. 97–106. Available at: http://network.icom.museum/fileadmin/user_upload/minisites/icofom/pdf/ISS%2040_ch_web2.pdf (Accessed: 7 January 2019).
Hogsden, C. and Poulter, E. K. (2012) 'The real other? Museum objects in digital contact networks', *Journal of Material Culture*, 17(3), pp. 265–286.
Iversen, O. S. and Smith, R. C. (2012) 'Scandinavian participatory design: Dialogic curation with teenagers', *Proceedings of the 11th international conference on interaction design and children*. ACM, pp. 106–115.
Jensen, O. and Richardson, T. (2004) *Making European space: Mobility, power and territorial identity*. London: Routledge.
Jewish Museum Berlin. (2018) *Jewish places*. Available at: www.jewish-places.de/ (Accessed: 2 November 2018).
Jewitt, C. (2012) 'Digital technologies in museums: New routes to engagement and participation', *Designs for Learning*, 5(1–2).
Kaiser, W., Krankenhagen, S. and Poehls, K. (2014) *Exhibiting Europe in museums: Transnational networks, collections, narratives, and representations*. Brooklyn, NY: Berghahn Books.
Kidd, J. (2012) 'The museum as narrative witness: Heritage performance and the production of narrative space', in Macleod, S., Hourston Hanks, L. and Hale, J. (eds.), *Museum making: Narratives, architectures, exhibitions*. Abingdon: Routledge, pp. 74–82.
Kohler-Koch, B. (2012) 'Post-Maastricht civil society and participatory democracy', *Journal of European Integration*, 34(7), pp. 809–824.
Krankenhagen, S. (2011) 'Exhibiting Europe: The development of European narratives in museums, collections, and exhibitions', *Culture Unbound: Journal of Current Cultural Research*, 3(3), pp. 269–278.

Levy, D. and Sznaider, N. (2002) 'Memory unbound: The holocaust and the formation of cosmopolitan memory', *European Journal of Social Theory*, 5(1), pp. 87–106.
Little, K. and Watson, I. (2015) 'Destination Tyneside – Stories of belonging: The philosophy and experience of developing a new permanent migration gallery at discovery museum in Newcastle upon Tyne', in Whitehead, C., Eckersley, S., Lloyd, K. and Mason R. (eds.), *Museums, migration and identity in Europe: Peoples, places and identities*. London: Routledge, pp. 183–206.
Lynch, B. (2014) '"Whose cake is it anyway?": Museums, civil society and the changing reality of public engagement', in *Museums and migration*. London: Routledge, pp. 81–94.
Mason, R., Whitehead, C. and Graham, H. (2013) 'One voice to many voices? Displaying polyvocality in an art gallery', in Golding, V. and Modest, W. (eds.), *Museums and communities: Curators, collections and collaboration*. London: Bloomsbury, pp. 163–177.
McLean, K. (1999) 'Museum exhibitions and the dynamics of dialogue', *Daedalus*, 128(3), pp. 83–107.
National Museum of American Jewish History. (n.d.) *Contemporary issues forum*. Available at: cif.nmajh.org (Accessed: 12 June 2018).
Noy, C. (2016) 'Participatory media and discourse in heritage museums: Co-constructing the public sphere?', *Communication, Culture & Critique*, 10(2), pp. 280–301.
Poehls, K. (2011) 'Europe, blurred: Migration, margins and the museum', *Culture Unbound: Journal of Current Cultural Research*, 3(3), pp. 337–353.
POLIN. (2016) *The Polish righteous*. Available at: https://sprawiedliwi.org.pl/en/ (Accessed: 2 November 2018).
POLIN. (2017) *Virtual shtetl*. Available at: https://sztetl.org.pl/en/ (Accessed: 2 November 2018).
Probst, L. (2003) 'Founding myths in Europe and the role of the holocaust', *New German Critique*, 90, pp. 45–58.
Pujol, L., Roussou, M., Poulo, S., Balet, O., Vayanou, M. and Ioannidis, Y. (2012) 'Personalizing interactive digital storytelling in archaeological museums: The CHESS project', in *40th annual conference of computer applications and quantitative methods in archaeology*. Amsterdam: Amsterdam University Press, pp. 77–90.
Ridge, M. (2014) *Crowdsourcing our cultural heritage*. Franham: Ashgate.
Rigney, A. (2012) 'Transforming memory and the European project', *New Literary History*, 43(4), pp. 607–628.
Sanders, E. and Stappers, P. J. (2008) 'Co-creation and the new landscapes of design', *Co-Design*, 4(1), pp. 5–18.
Schuler, D. and Namioka, A. (eds.). (1993) *Participatory design: Principles and practices*. Hillsdale: Laurence Erlbaum Associates.
Simon, N. (2008) *The participatory museum*. Santa Cruz: Museum 2.0.
Skorton, D. (2017) 'Trusted sources: Why museums and libraries are more relevant than ever', *Smithsonian Insider*.
Smith, L., Wetherell, M. and Campbell, G. (2018) *Emotion, affective practices, and the past in the present*. London and New York: Routledge.

Smørdal, O., Stuedahl, D. and Sem, I. (2014) 'Experimental zones: Two cases of exploring frames of participation in a dialogic museum', *Digital Creativity*, 3, pp. 224–232.

Tchen, J.K.W. (1992) 'Creating a dialogic museum: The Chinatown history museum experiment' in Karp, I., Kreamer, C.M. and Lavine, S. D. (eds.) *Museums and communities: The politics of public culture*. Washington DC: Smithsonian Institution Press, pp. 285–326.

Vassos, S. et al. (2016) 'Art-Bots: Toward chat-based conversational experiences in museums', in Nack F., Gordon A. (eds.) *Interactive Storytelling. ICIDS 2016*. New York: Springer, pp. 433–437.

Witcomb, A. (2003) *Re-imagining the museum: Beyond the mausoleum*. London and New York: Routledge.

Witcomb, A. (2015) 'Toward a pedagogy of feeling: Understanding how museums create a space for cross-cultural encounters', in *The international handbooks of museum studies*. Chichester: Wiley-Blackwell, pp. 321–344.

Wong, A. (2011) 'Ethical issues of social media in museums: A case study', *Museum Management and Curatorship*, 26(2), pp. 97–112.

Wyman, B., Smith, S., Meyers, D. and Godfrey, M. (2011) 'Digital storytelling in museums: Observations and best practices', *Curator: The Museum Journal*, 54(4), pp. 461–468.

Artefact vignette #1: *Transformation Machine*

Annelie Berner, Monika Halina Seyfried, Gabi Arrigoni and Areti Galani

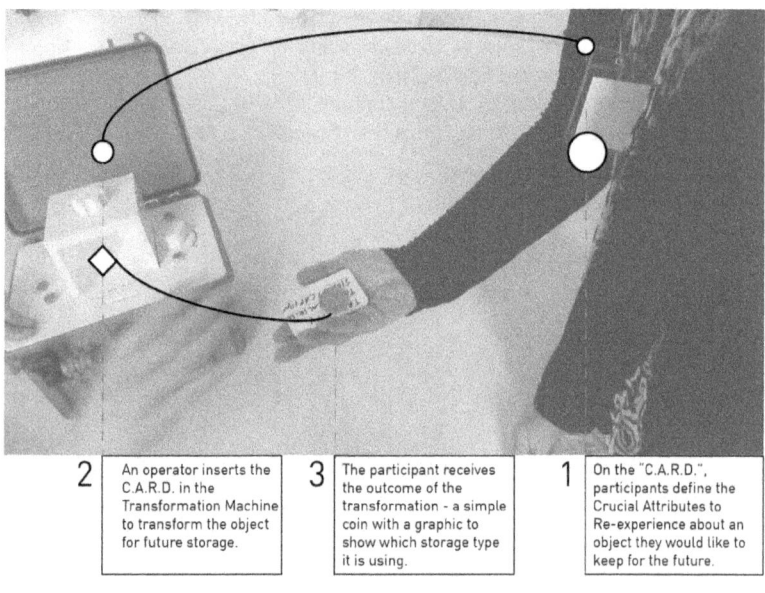

2. An operator inserts the C.A.R.D. in the Transformation Machine to transform the object for future storage.

3. The participant receives the outcome of the transformation - a simple coin with a graphic to show which storage type it is using.

1. On the "C.A.R.D.", participants define the Crucial Attributes to Re-experience about an object they would like to keep for the future.

The *Transformation Machine* is a speculative artefact that enables people to see how their perspective on European heritage might alter the holdings of vast museum databases. It was created as part of a 'futurescaping' workshop for museum professionals to explore the scenario of deleting a significant part of European museums' collections to respond more closely to the evolving notion of 'European-ness' and its constantly changing values. The curators-participants in the workshop were assigned fictitious roles as members of a fictional *Deletion Bureau*. Subsequently, they were asked to feed an artificial intelligence (A.I.) a set of keywords associated with key features of artefacts selected from the collections in their own institutions.

Trained upon the keywords, the A.I. device would then learn how to discard collection items that were no longer relevant. The *Transformation Machine* subverted the process of deletion, turning it into a transformative one. The machine gave the option to participants to reduce the discarded objects into a small token containing only a limited set of crucial attributes from the original (e.g. its texture or its association with a specific historical event). The transformation machine introduces a shift from the binary alternative between preservation and deletion by suggesting a mid-way solution as a means for preserving only the features deemed to be significant and contributing to the definition of the artefact as an expression of European-ness. This design experiment addresses the complexity of meanings, values and criteria for defining heritage. While abstract questions can be posed such as what a collection should represent or how it should place itself for a strategic vision of the future, the *Transformation Machine* required participants to physically enact such decision-making, to visualise and experience the impact of their decisions. In this intervention, suspension of disbelief and material engagement with a fictional object supports a process of negotiation and decision-making that generates dialogue and opportunities for collective thinking and sharing concerns, a space for openness and constant readjustment of vision and collective positioning. It proposes, therefore, that digital transformation should be treated as a site for productive dialogue and re-imagining of cultural heritage rather than a source of techno-determined utopian and dystopian heritage futures.

The context of the *Transformation Machine*: www.cohere-4.com/future scaping/2018/3/5/futurescaping-workshop

Acknowledgements

The *Transformation Machine* was created through a collaboration between researchers in the Copenhagen Institute of Interaction Design (CIID) and Media, Culture, Heritage at Newcastle University, UK. Our thanks go to all our colleagues who supported this process. We would like to thank Peter Kuhberg of indsigt.design for physical design. This research was carried out as part of the project CoHERE (2016–2019), which has received funding from the European Union Horizon 2020 programme under grant agreement NO 693289.

4 Participation and dialogue

Curatorial reflexivity in participatory processes

Dagny Stuedahl, Torhild Skåtun, Ageliki Lefkaditou and Tobias Messenbrink

Introduction

Lately, several museum projects in the Nordic countries and around the world have explored the potential of extending museum participation into actively involving users in the process of museum exhibition design. This participatory museum paradigm shift (Holdgaard and Klastrup, 2014) defines visitors as collaborators, who bring into the museum design process diverse knowledge, expectations and experiences. The aims of this active visitor involvement are multiple and include the pragmatics of shaping relevant activities as a political endeavour of democratising cultural heritage institutions. This new situation raises key reflections for museums such as (a) how museum professionals co-produce knowledge in dialogue with museum users, (b) how museums may develop infrastructures that embrace participatory methods in ways that are meaningful to diverse visitor groups, and (c) how museums may fulfil the role of open cultural heritage institutions as places for social change, dialogue, democracy, human rights and activism (see e.g. Black, 2010; Marstine, 2011; Message, 2006; Sandell, 2016). This is a matter of how museums and museum professionals constitute their sites as organisations for public dialogue and participation, rather than as institutions that merely exhibit objects (Lynch, 2011; Parry, 2007; Phillips, 2003).

The participatory museum paradigm comes in parallel with the 'turn to openness' currently going on in cultural heritage institutions, which includes aspects of sociability and designability (Marttila and Botero, 2013). Openness requires dialogue and participation, and being attentive to what visitors know and how that knowledge may change the institution. Visitor involvement establishes connections with audience groups that go beyond the 'boundary encounter' practices (Meyer, 2010) employed when, for example, amateurs are mobilised in collecting cultural heritage objects (Star and Griesemer, 1989). Participatory processes create relations that help museum professionals to attune to their visitors' interests. Rather than being understood as activities related to content, visitor participation has been framed as a knowledge process that connects museum staff with societal issues, and as a method to open up museum exhibition design to views and preferences of the audience (Stuedahl and Smørdal, 2015).

The encounter with visitor groups or stakeholders as participants in a collaborative process requires dialogue that goes beyond conversation by involving certain qualities in which 'participants display ability to listen, to be empathic and to open up to others' argument and show a willingness to change their standpoint' (Dysthe, Bernhardt and Esbjørn, 2013, p. 51; Linell, 2009). Our understanding of dialogue is, therefore, closely related to active participation and leans on how Norwegian professor in educational research Olga Dysthe links Bakhtin's theoretical tradition of dialogue, which emphasises the multivoicedness of dialogue (see e.g. Bakhtin, 1981) with existential philosophy. It is always 'We' and not 'I' who create meaning through dialogic interactions. The other inspiration for our concept of dialogue is the Brazilian educator Paolo Freire's political pedagogy. For him, dialogue was the starting point for consciousness-raising, which would lead to change (Dysthe, Bernhardt and Esbjørn, 2013; Freire, 1970). The third is John Dewey's pragmatic approach to knowledge, as constructed in practical activities in which groups cooperate within a cultural context (Dewey, 1934, 2007).

In this chapter, we discuss how museum professionals engage dialogue when integrating participatory approach, methods and tools into their participatory practice. We describe a participatory design (PD) process related to the exhibition *FOLK – from racial types to DNA sequences (FOLK)*, which opened at the Norwegian Museum of Science and Technology (NTM) in March 2018. The participatory project involved a group of 11 young people 12 to 18 years old from a multi-ethnic suburban area of Oslo. The participatory project was centred on developing a digital activity connected to the exhibition. Before coming to the museum, the young people had already been members of Grorud Youth Council, a district advisory body which advises on community issues. The participatory process was managed by a participatory team within the museum, consisting of one curator, a museum pedagogue and one interaction designer from the exhibition team together with a researcher from a partner university. The participatory team planned the workshops and collectively facilitated them on the basis of their various competences. The participatory process lasted for a period of ten months and included eight workshops. The data collected in the PD process were recorded during the workshops by the authors and participatory team. The video and audio files, alongside reflection notes and written diaries, were shared within the team. Between the workshops, we communicated with the participants on Facebook (FB). We used a closed FB group to share not only plans for each workshop but also tips for sound-databases, editing

64 *Dagny Stuedahl et al.*

tools and so forth. This chapter is based on analysis of these recordings and notes and emphasises the development of purpose, the new judgements, understanding (dis)continuities of participatory practices and the adjustment of practice between each workshop.

The exhibition *FOLK* explores historical and contemporary research on human biological diversity through its interactions with society, culture and politics. The curatorial research interweaves understandings of individual and group identities with broader political and ethical issues, such as concerns on migration, the rise of racist and discriminatory attitudes or indigenous peoples' rights. Therefore, the topics of science, identity and belonging were the starting point for the participatory team, which focused on the making of a visitor activity. Parallel to this participatory process, the exhibition team organised multiple encounters with focus-group workshops, public lectures and roundtables. All these meetings aimed at fostering dialogue between museum professionals and individuals or social groups outside the museum, and at creating communal spaces on a topic with difficult history and high contemporary societal relevance to Norway and more broadly to Europe. Here, we focus on the process of the ten months collaboration and co-creation in the participatory project.

The outcome, a digital installation inviting museum visitors to mix, record and edit sounds that express the diversity of human emotions, was placed at the entrance of the *FOLK* exhibition (Figure 4.1). The installation was given the title *The Sound of FOLK*, which reflects the exhibition title, *FOLK – from racial types to DNA sequences*. Almost all museum visitors, alone or in groups, encounter the digital installation when entering the museum. It invites adults and children to listen and create soundscapes describing an emotion they choose out of eight categories. The soundscape they produce, for example, a soundmix of an ambulance siren, a baby crying and a sigh expressing the emotion fear, is uploaded to an archive, together with a written text and a picture or an avatar that describes the sound. The sound installation aims to strengthen the dialogue among visitors, by either creating soundscapes together or by listening to other people's contributions on the tablets or under the sound shower. During the formal learning activities, the installation is used to connect with the exhibition themes on human biological similarities and differences. The students are asked to explore the exhibition and make a soundscape that expresses an emotion connected to an object of their choice. The educator uses these stories of sound, for example, of how a poster from an human zoo in London in the 1830s elicits sadness or surprise, to facilitate dialogues around the exhibition topic.

The chapter addresses the relationship between co-production of the installation and dialogue with participants in the participatory process. We focus on three levels and three forms of dialogue that the participatory

Participation and dialogue 65

Figure 4.1 The digital installation *The sound of FOLK*.

Note: *The Sound of FOLK* was developed during the participatory process. The museum staff collaborated with a group of 11 young participants over a period of ten months. The installation is placed close to the entrance of the exhibition *FOLK*.

Source: Photo: Håkon Bergseth.

team engaged in. These dialogic practices were necessary to retain the commitment and motivation of the young participants while ensuring that the design process developed according to the time frame of the exhibition process. The three levels of dialogue refer to the actors involved, who took part and from what positions. The participatory team managed dialogues with:

- The young participants during the workshops and in between the workshops.
- The participatory team summarising the workshops and planning the next steps of the process.
- The main exhibition team, reporting from the participatory process and adjusting decisions on content, form and levels of communication on the basis of the work with the young participants.

The dialogues were both discursive and practice based, as the encounters in the participatory process were based both on discussions of concepts and on experiences of diversity and identity, as well as on collaborative and creative activities. We have organised the forms of dialogue in three axes:

- Discursive; discussions, narratives, conceptual mapping and conceptual clarifications.
- Collaborative and creative activities, media production, model building and so forth.
- Voting, testing and evaluating on material outcomes.

Our analysis in the chapter focuses on how these levels and axes of dialogue were sources of the museum professionals' reflection and reflexivity that was crucial for grasping and supporting the participatory process. The research question we draw attention to is: what are the main challenges of making dialogues work, and what reflections are created during participatory and co-productive processes in museum exhibitions? The chapter focuses on the dialogic work and reflections of the museum staff involved in the participatory team.

Co-production, dialogue and reflection in the participatory museum paradigm

Audience participants' involvement in exhibition design requires creating a shared and neutral space for both museum staff and non-museum employees (Mygind, Hällman and Bentsen, 2015). Many participatory museum projects fail to overcome institutional power structures and relations and the result of the process is controlled by the museum (Lynch and Alberti, 2010). Participation and dialogue thus is a matter of museum professionals appropriating participatory methods adjusted to the situated context of the museum, the topic of the exhibition, the participants and the communities in question. This appropriation is a matter of translations – of re-ordering relations and 'drawing things together' (Björgvinsson, Ehn and Hillgren, 2012; Suchman, 2002). It necessitates temporal and transformative processes of finding new ways to make judgements, to understand (dis)continuities and to adjust practice. Participatory processes in museums, as in other organisations and institutions, include processes of staff becoming participatory designers through enactments, dialogues, collaborative learning and understanding. This is a process of becoming, where matters of concern relate to appropriation of participatory methods and its outcome (Stuedahl and Smørdal, 2015). These processes are strengthened if the organisational infrastructures support this becoming, which is not always the case (Dindler and Iversen, 2014; Pihkala, 2018; Saad-Sulonen et al., 2018).

Participation and dialogue 67

Visitor participation in museum exhibition design is also a form of co-production. Helen Graham argues that this co-production tries to overcome the access barrier of the glass case of the exhibited museum object by expanding the variety of people and objects that are involved in museum practice (Graham, 2016). Graham illustrates how this expansion by co-production collides with the stabilisation processes needed for museums to legitimate their work. Co-production, participation and community involvement in museums in this way challenge the limits of the glass case exhibitionary complex (Bennett, 2006), and the museum performs simultaneously 'the desire to expand the number of people involved, while seeking to retain, and even stabilise, museums' political assumptions' (Graham, 2016, p. 4). This double move of pluralisation and stabilisation can become problematic. It questions the assumption that museums' legitimacy necessarily originates from making 'objects' publicly accessible through display rather than by cultivating responsive and reciprocal relationships with specific people and community groups (Graham, Mason and Nayling, 2013). Museums, Graham suggests, could benefit from adopting *relational ontologies* rather than particularity or abstraction. This includes viewing participation as a way to conceptualise the relational state of things, people and events in participatory processes. It also includes viewing *translations* as a concept that captures the dialogues and interpretation work involved in participation (Graham, 2016; Latour, 2005; Treimo, in press). Graham's insight into the double move between expansion of knowledge perspectives and stabilisation of museum legitimacy gives an indication of what goes on behind the scenes of museum participatory processes and dialogues with visitor groups.

Participatory practice, dialogue and co-production of exhibitions require embracing uncertainty, which is often experienced as in conflict with the needs for certainty built into the operating values of the museum (Morse, Macpherson and Robinson, 2013). The challenges are multiple; participatory practices go beyond the competencies of the museum professionals, where dialogues have traditionally been mediated by the exhibition or in guiding tours. Participatory practices require an often-missing shared organisational strategy and a proactive plan for managing cultural differences between staff, visitors and societal context. Further, participatory practices require acceptance to partial submission of authority by museum staff, as well as aligning personal agendas and emotions according to Mygind (Mygind, Hällman and Bentsen, 2015). Acceptance may bridge the gaps between intentions and realities of dialogues and co-production between museum professionals and participating visitors, but requires awareness of how one's own analytic framework influences interpretation and actions. This requires reflection and reflexivity.

Reflections during the design process has been the central topic of Donald Schön's (1987) argument for understanding design as a reflective process. Schön has been studying professional designers in several domains to articulate common elements in their practices. He states that designers' knowledge differs from everyday actions because designers reflect in action; the designer may even respond by reflection in action; by thinking about what she is doing while she is doing it, in such a way as to influence further doing (Schön, 1987). This gives us an interesting departure point for discussions on participatory design in museums, as it turns the focus towards museum staffs' reflection on procedural activities in addition to objects and artefacts.

Sociological and anthropological literature abounds with defences of, and challenges to, reflexivity. It is impossible to do justice to such rich insights in this limited space, so here we will attempt only to sketch how central methodological concerns on reflexive interpretation in the social sciences resonate with the practice of understanding in participatory museum exhibition design, as well as in other participatory projects. Reflexivity has gained much currency through a renewed interest in the sociological work of Pierre Bourdieu and his focus on undermining dualisms such as objectivism/subjectivism and structure/agent (e.g. Bourdieu and Wacquant, 1992; Bourdieu, 2000). Weber differentiates between being reflective and reflexive in research as a matter of whether one focuses on scrutinising 'the assumptions, biases, and perspectives that underlie one specific component of our research' or 'all components of our research, and in particular the interrelationships among them', respectively (Weber, 2003, p. vi). While the part of being reflective resembles what Schön calls reflection-in-action, being reflexive relates not only to the researchers' own process but also on how they are situated in a context where both their research arena, institutional relations and disciplinary background play a role in their work. In this case, reflexivity allows the reflection-in-action to include analysis of how contextual relations influence the design work.

However, there is also a difference between reflexivity in research and reflexivity in design. Research has developed tools for studying and describing, whereas in design, these tools do not fully support the work of creating new design objects. 'Design is intentional; therefore, design interpretations are also intentional. It is intention that predisposes us towards certain data and values. This means that interpretation cannot be done without an understanding of a direction – without desiderata' (Nelson and Stolterman, 2003, p. 156). Nelson and Stolterman (2003) suggest that even in the most objective approaches in design, such as engineering design, there is still a need for interpretation:

> Interpretation, as a part of the design process, serves the same purpose as evidence and proof does in science. Interpretation is part of our

Participation and dialogue 69

attempt to grasp the conditions and context that exist and will set the stage for our ideas and new design.

(p. 154)

The concept of interpretation with a direction gives a special character to the dialogue and reflexivity in a participatory design process (Stuedahl, 2004). Implementing a reflexive methodology in PD design means, therefore, to be aware of the intentionality behind interpretations and translations in dialogues. This reflexivity also includes the theoretical, disciplinary and institutional context of intentions and interpretations.

Participatory design competencies in museums as reflection-in-action

In participatory design (PD), facilitating participatory processes requires knowledge and structures that support the open-ended process of continuous dialogue and co-creation between designers and external participants (Björgvinsson, Ehn and Hillgren, 2012; Ehn, 2008; Dantec and DiSalvo, 2013; Hillgren, Seravalli and Emilson, 2011). It is important to focus on the designer using the method, and on that we cannot know participatory methods without the person or people enacting them (Light and Akama, 2012). This includes the practitioner's characteristics, the worldviews, purpose and decisions made on the way, as well as the moment-by-moment dialogues and shifts in position, focus and delivery that form the fundamental elements of PD facilitation.

Schön's reflective concept described the process of the designing as a conversation with situations: in a good process of design, the conversation with the situation is reflective. In response to the situation's back-talk, the designer reflects in two ways: reflection-on-action and reflection-in-action. Reflection-on-action is a retrospective on the construction of the problem, the strategies of actions or on the model of the phenomena, and may have been implicit in the designer's moves (Schön, 1987). The designer's reflection-in-action is interpreted as reflection during the design process. The understanding involved in the reflection-in-action is defined by changing activities: 'the unique and uncertain situation comes to be understood through the attempt to change it, and changed through the attempt to understand it' (Schön, 1987, p. 132). For museum professionals working in PD processes, reflection-in-action may revolve around understanding how participants engage – or not – in a collaborative process, and changing activities according to the development process.

In the museum context, reflection-in-action is about trying to grasp the participants' understanding of the project. Users' or participants' interpretation and understanding may differ from museum staff's. The museum staff should be able to take the users' understanding as their departure point: 'by taking the meaning of Others as a fundamental starting point for design, designers must proceed from their understanding of users' understanding, which is understanding of understanding, or second-order understanding' (Krippendorf, 1995, p. 149). In participatory museum exhibition design, this brings awareness to how curators develop the competencies needed for analysing plurality and complexities, reflecting on these and conveying these into strategies of exhibition design.

The shifting of perspectives is a characteristic of dialogic practices, as dialogue requires reflexivity and positionality in the 'We', which both assume that the participants in dialogue are aware of their position and are prepared for this to be negotiated. Facilitation of shifting perspectives in PD is a competency which can be achieved only in dialogic practice and is what we have earlier framed as 'matters of becoming' (Pihkala, 2018; Stuedahl and Smørdal, 2015). This dialogic practice includes front stage (e.g. workshops) and back stage relations; exploring, creating and consolidating working relationships; creating attention and support around an exhibition topic; and investing time in dialogue with participants in order to build common understanding (Dindler and Iversen, 2014). The dialogic perspective requires an emergent lens to the participatory processes as well as to the institutional patterns and practices in museums to be able to connect the diverging purposes and focus involved in participatory processes (Arnstein, 1969).

The challenge is to find the tools and techniques for dialogue and awareness, which enable the voices of the participants to be valued at a level equal to that of the museum professionals (Tzibazi, 2013; Stuedahl and Skåtun, 2018). Giving authority and legitimacy to young audience groups in the design process may challenge the professionalism of the museum professionals if they are not seeing the intentions of dialogue, negotiation and critique as a means of developing meaningful alternatives (Smith and Iversen, 2014). A participatory approach that includes audience in the curatorial process, such as in the conceptual, operational and evaluation phases of exhibition design, would also require a common agenda and integrated methods on all levels of the museum organisation (Taxén, 2004). However, a common agenda can have different meanings to the different participants involved.

Making PD at the museum dialogic

When the museum participatory team engaged in the co-production project, they kept dialogues cross-axes of departments and disciplines, responsibilities and interests. The participatory team reported to the exhibition group

Participation and dialogue 71

consisting of 17 museum professionals and an external designer, while 30 experts and students joined in during the two-year exhibition development. To this aim, the participatory team was established consisting of curator, educator, interaction designer and researcher. The curator had to report and *legitimise the participatory process*, both towards the exhibition project group and to the museum management. While the exhibition group recognised the importance of long engagement to increase ownership of the participatory process and interweave different perspectives, the participatory process with the young people started at a point when curatorial themes were beginning to settle. Therefore, the participatory team experienced more pressure when arguing for the open-ended nature of the participatory process. As the curator recollects:

> We do not think that the management level really knew in detail what we were working on. They knew we had invited a group of young people from Grorud but not how it was organised and facilitated. The exhibition project group had good insight in the process, and gave their consent, but they still only had the knowledge we translated.
>
> (interview with curator Ageliki Lefkaditou)

The curator argued for the participatory process as a way to research peoples' opinions (and experiences) on the topic of human diversity and belonging, and to expand the scopes and perspectives on content, form and communication in the exhibition.

The aim of the participatory team was to work with a group of young people who had a special interest in the exhibition topic. At the same time, the team wished to avoid the common approach of representation as a starting point for participation in projects under the auspices of intercultural dialogue policies and initiatives, and thus single out the specific groups as multicultural youths. The participatory team made contact with Grorud Youth Council, a youth organisation in the Grorud suburb of Oslo, through a youth umbrella organisation. The organisation had a special attention towards active citizenship and youth participation on several levels in society. The Grorud district is a multicultural residential area with among 50% immigrant citizens, consisting of first-, second- and third-generation immigrants. The six boys and four girls, from 13 to 18 years, who came to the first museum workshop had various backgrounds, and a common engagement and consciousness of being a young person in a multicultural district.

The facilitation of roundtable dialogues was shared within the team, and facilitation of collaborative dialogues in workshop activities was distributed among team members throughout the eight workshops, which we present later on in this section (Figure 4.2). After each workshop, the participatory

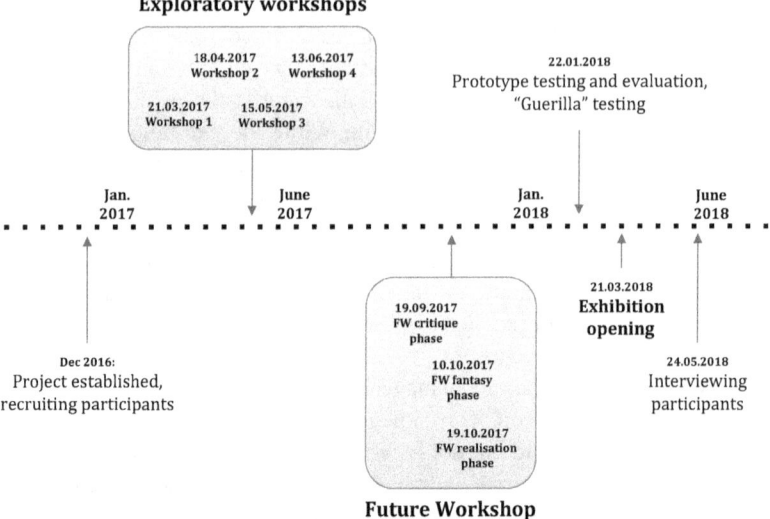

Figure 4.2 The participatory process of *The Sound of FOLK* lasted over eight workshops.
Source: Illustration: Tobias Messenbrink (2018).

team debriefed on the outcome of the workshop, and discussed next steps in the continuation of both the participatory process and the design.

In the PD meetings with the young people, the museum participatory team struggled to grasp the participatory practice and to redefine their roles related to the open-ended character of the process. They started with several potential design outcomes – an exhibition activity, an educational activity or an installation – and had to make sure that diverse professional agendas, responsibilities, demands for certainty concerning time, human resources and funding were aligned. While they had to be focused on the outcome of the PD process, they were also responsible for keeping the participatory process open, given the uncertainty of how the young participants would understand the complex topic and content of the exhibition.

The participatory team decided to focus on a sound activity that created the opportunity for audience creation and contribution to the exhibition, while avoiding privacy concerns. The team argued that sound would complement the predominantly visual communication of human biological diversity prioritised in the exhibition. We *see* difference, but what does *hearing* difference entail? This double focus on exploring a new medium – sound – and its potential for participatory activities, as well as on grasping young people's

Participation and dialogue 73

understanding of science, identity and belonging, formed the basis for the eight workshops of the participatory process. The first three workshops concentrated on the young people's literacy with sound and narratives of identity and belonging. The dialogues were facilitated through concept mapping, and the production of audio dramas showed the diversity of descriptions and the blending of cultural and biological markers of the young participants' identities. The group discussions focused predominantly on how cultural understandings of similarity and difference are embedded in everyday contexts. However, in the debriefing sessions, the challenges identified were multiple. The museum professionals reflected on the process being too open, and that the link to the exhibition theme became too vague. They worried that dialogues on such a complex topic without having the actual exhibit open may be too demanding for the participants. They also recognised that while most of the young people were well-versed in discussing issues related to racism, discrimination or belonging, they had problems relating such considerations to the *role of science*. Still, the team agreed that working in an open-ended manner also had a purpose of giving insights into how young people from a multicultural district reflected in words and actions about identity and belonging, as well as on how they would like to engage with these issues in a museum. This would have not been accessible in other ways.

The fourth workshop focused on presenting the exhibition work and the collaborative production of stories related to defined objects chosen for the exhibition. Nevertheless, after the fourth workshop, the participatory team still struggled with the open-ended process and became uncertain of the young people's engagement. One critical reflection was that the participants took a student role and delivered assignments and responded as if they were in school. They still had very little understanding of what a museum activity (or a museum practice!) is, and it was challenging for them to envisage how an unfamiliar topic could be communicated in an unfamiliar space. Faced with these challenges, the participatory team decided to change strategy. They put more emphasis on collaborative dialogues and activities related to developing a prototype focusing on identity and belonging.

The team decided to try the Future Workshop (FW) method in the fifth participatory workshop. This is a method developed in the 1970s by Robert Jungk, Ruediger Lutz and Norbert R. Muellert (Vidal, 2005) to facilitate group-dialogues and find solutions to social problems in urban planning projects. The method was developed especially for people without experience in creative processes and consists of five phases: *preparation phase, critique phase, phantasy phase, realisation phase* and *evaluation phase*. The FW was adjusted to the participatory process, and the team decided to focus on the critique phase, phantasy phase, realisation phase and evaluation

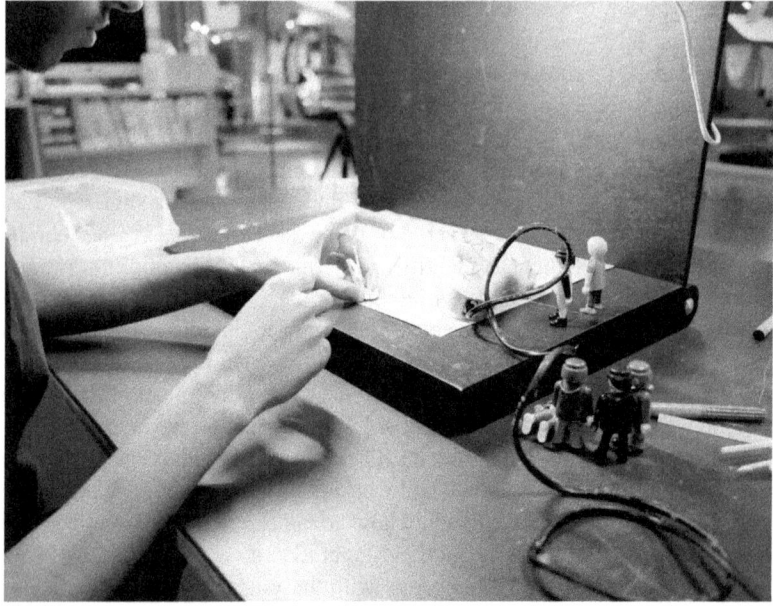

Figure 4.3 Future Workshop, the phantasy phase.
Source: Photo: Tobias Messenbrink.

phase. The participatory team redefined the previous four exploratory workshops as being the preparation phase. The facilitation of participatory workshops was also discussed, and it was decided to have one clear facilitator for each session. The educator would lead the fifth workshop. The design researcher would facilitate the phantasy phase, while the sound designer would be responsible for the realisation phase and prototype testing in workshop seven. This choice reflected a need for structuring the process, and start focusing on a final design outcome and a product that would be reliable.

For the critique phase in workshop five, the whole participatory project group visited the exhibition *Typical* at the Intercultural Museum in Oslo. The exhibition used a variety of interactive installations and textual statements to examine the concept of prejudice. This topic resonated with the themes the participatory team tried to raise in the previous discussions with the young people. During the visit, the young participants and museum professionals discussed experiences with different forms of exhibition engagement with the topic in this specific exhibition.

Workshop six, phantasy phase, focused on drawing a picture of future possibilities. It took place in the makerspace at the museum and the participants

Participation and dialogue 75

worked in groups of three, involving museum staff and young participants. Each group developed a scenario for a potential museum visit that made use of sound and touched upon the themes of identity and belonging. A range of materials was available to enact their scenarios on a small wooden stage. The dialogic collaboration levelled the power relations between participants and museums professionals, as dialogue was easier while collaborating and looking down at a stage than by making eye-to-eye contact around a table. The group engaged in a long discussion on the kind of sounds used in the installation, and what they would express. They decided that the installation would invite people to reflect on the connections between sounds and emotions with individual and cultural identities and thus offer another view on human similarities and differences. An FB vote was arranged to decide which model would be developed further in workshop seven, the realisation phase. A prototype of the installation, based on the FB voting session, was discussed in workshop eight, the evaluation phase.

Dialogues and reflections during and after the participatory process

The dialogues and reflections that emerged during the participatory process can be explored on the basis of Graham's dilemma between pluralisation and stability. We suggest that this could be seen as a dialogic process of changing standpoints, listening and being emphatic and open to the multivoiced arguments of the participants. Our experience suggests that stabilisation comes through continual adjustment. The awareness of this complexity in roles and movement through dialogic reflection-in-action allowed the participatory process to move forward.

Keeping the process open was a strategic choice, despite the challenges it elicited for the participants and for the main exhibition group. This openness required that the participatory process was discussed and evaluated constantly in relation to the multivocality that the participants brought in, as well as the needs of the exhibition group. The reflection-in-action that the participatory team made during, and after, in de-briefing dialogues, was focused on how to organise the dialogue with the young participants as well as with the exhibition group and the topic of the exhibition.

Reflections on participatory dialogue, engagement and adjustment of method

Much of the reflection-in-action of the participatory team centred on the dialogue with the young participants and their engagement in the participatory process. The thematic refocusing of the process from an emphasis on scientific perspectives to familiar, everyday situations and the structuring of the whole design process around the participants' interest in the medium of sound were the most important strategic changes to ensure the participants' continuous engagement.

The participatory team was also concerned with creating an environment that would empower the participants. This required being empathic to both the young participants' experiences of the museum space and the participatory process. All workshops took place in a room dedicated to experimental exhibition making outside of museum working hours, which meant that the young people did not get to experience the museum in full activity. However, the workshops started with joint dinner and conversation on more general topics to enhance the feeling of safety and common purpose. The participatory team noticed that the young people quickly became familiar with the space and seemed comfortable and safe.

The participatory team discussed whether an alignment of motivations was needed to maintain the participants' engagement. The museum professionals aligned around the common purpose of creating a participatory activity, but the participatory team wanted to address more emphatically what the benefit could be for the young people. Therefore, they prioritised presenting the museum exhibition process and revealing different aspects of working in a museum. Some of the young participants expressed that coming to the museum in the evening gave them a feeling of belonging to a valued group and that their views were important.

The introduction of the Future Workshop (FW) method gave all participants a common and structured understanding of the outcomes of each workshop and introduced a methodological framework that assigned equal roles to the participatory team and the participants. It also legitimated the continuation of the time-consuming participatory process towards the museum exhibition team, by adding a concrete, acknowledged scientific method to the process. The dialogues during the workshops became more structured and the participatory team could focus more on ensuring engagement than struggling with uncertainty on all levels. In this sense, the FW method became a stabilising factor that allowed pluralisation.

By the end of the process, the participants were pleased to see that their ideas materialised in the installation. They also expressed that the participatory process gave them insight into the workings of a museum and an understanding of the complex processes of exhibition making. The museum had no previous established strategy for community participation or dealing with cultural diversity. While not foregrounded during the process, the museum professionals worked on opening up a discussion about diversity at the museum and arranged to hire some of the young people as explainers

Participation and dialogue 77

during the summer season. These outcomes point to how reflexivity on the whole participatory process may affect engagement during the process itself and beyond it.

Dialogue and reflections of the outcome of the participatory project

The slow shift in how the participatory project engaged with the exhibition's topic required reconfiguring the project's contribution to the exhibition. The activity with the sound installation focused on identity and belonging and was complementary to exhibition themes but did not reproduce them. The sound installation could encourage interaction and dialogue, allowing visitors to experience an easier and familiar entry to the exhibition that is more demanding and dense in content. As the time of the exhibition opening was approaching and the whole exhibition group was becoming anxious to see the outcomes of the participatory process, stabilising this aspect of alternative entry became important.

The participatory group realised, however, that while the theme of the exhibition was becoming easier to grasp in the sound installation, its connection and contribution to the exhibition's topic appeared weaker and more abstract. A reason for this may be that the user-generated soundscape was not integrated as part of the exhibition narrative (Galani and Moschovi, 2013). When the sound designer presented the prototype to the exhibition team, they suggested a number of adjustments to create visual coherence with the exhibition and to showcase the different ways humans express their emotions on human diversity.

The new relationship to the exhibition, however, led to another strategic translation regarding the spatial relations between the exhibition and the installation. During the Future Workshop (FW) process, the participatory team had to consider the best position for the installation to open reflections and dialogue on the exhibition topic, the limitations of space within the exhibition, and the request of the exhibition's designer to keep the room contemplative. An interactive activity based on sound did not align well with the overall atmosphere of the show.

The participatory team responded to these new challenges by experimentally placing the activity at the foyer space of the museum. For this decision, they relied on recent museum research, which points to the multiple transformative functions of the foyer space (Laursen, Kristiansen and Drotner, 2016). While this decision was motivated by the intention to prepare the visitors through a broader and more familiar topic, the response from the visitors was lower than expected. Therefore, the activity was finally moved right outside the exhibition entrance.

78 *Dagny Stuedahl et al.*

Dialogue and reflections on the exhibition topic in the participatory project

The participatory team tried several times during the four first workshops to open up an explicit dialogue about how science interacts with conceptions of identity and belonging through the concepts of race and ethnicity. This seemed to engage the young participants less than discussions on daily life and their own experiences with identity and belonging. The initial theme made more sense to the experts, and the participatory team reflected extensively on whether they should insist more on focusing on science.

For example, while the curator noticed that a commercial DNA testing kit attracted the participants' interest and could become a good entry point for discussing issues related to nature and nurture, she did not bring it back to the dialogue. This was a result of inexperience and fear of dominating the discussion, as well as a conscious choice to follow on what emerged as more relevant for the participants. The participatory team decided that they were not interested in replicating the voice of the exhibition, but in embracing other perspectives even if they appeared to be leading astray from the original themes.

The title of the participatory project, *Science, Identity, and Belonging*, did not change in any of the documents or in the group's social media account. Even if the focus on science became less obvious, this reflected the wish of the participatory team to hold on to it as a possibility. Meanwhile, for the curator, the introduction of the Future Workshop (FW) process gave the focus on scientific practices a return, but in another, more subtle, form. The FW introduced a scientific method of structured experimentation, and the focus on science was translated into a focus on scientific method:

> With the FW solution, that's where we left the original focus on science and moved to the idea towards emotions expressing the themes of diversity, identity and belonging. However, we engaged with conscious experimentation. Though we left science, our method became more scientific: By experimenting with FW as a method of inquiry, we established an experimental zone, we became co-researchers and even redefined our research questions.
> (interview with curator Ageliki Lefkaditou)

Finally, the participatory team redefined the focus on science, society and culture – after consultation with the whole exhibition group – without changing the design outcome. For example, they translated the number of categories of emotions available for the visitors to create soundscapes to be related to research in social psychology and anthropology of emotions

Participation and dialogue 79

and a critical positioning (Messenbrink, 2018). The participatory team also discussed if the re-focus resonated with research on the role of emotions in constructing group identities, belonging and origins as well as in processes of racialisation, discrimination and exclusion, to be found in social scientific research.

Concluding thoughts

This chapter explores how reflection and dialogue during participatory processes enable museum professionals to sustain engagement and to make translations necessary for exhibition design on difficult topics such as belonging and identity for young individuals with diverse backgrounds in Norway/Europe. While an exhibition design process requires a final product within given institutional frames and deadlines, co-production and multiple voices flourish with openness and investment in long-term processes. Our research suggests that this tension between stabilisation and pluralisation is a creative one. Reflection-in-action over the whole participatory design (PD) process allowed the museum professionals to acknowledge that stabilisation is only momentary and in dialogue with continued movement. The explicit discussions of the challenges that the topic posed for the participants brought an awareness of the complexity of roles, motivations and agendas in the participatory process and made it possible for the museum professionals to reflect on reasons for what the participants could contribute and what they could not.

When the interdisciplinary participatory team embarked on this project, they were faced with an unfamiliar practice and the lack of supporting arguments for PD at the museum. They struggled with establishing shared understandings and language, with achieving participatory methods, situations and actions, as well as with being reflexive and ready to negotiate and change their perspectives. The PD process required adjustments in methods, in relation to the main exhibition, and ultimately in the prevalence of the specific exhibition topic in the outcome of the participatory project. It is through these translations and re-configurations that the museum professionals became participatory designers able to assemble, justify and defend the PD process.

Participation emerged through the appropriation of PD methods, tools and techniques, while the museum professionals benefited from the latter in terms of translating both purpose and supporting arguments for the participatory process. Within the PD process, different levels and forms of dialogue – among nested groups of actors and covering a range of discursive and creative activities – sharpened the interpretative skills of the museum professionals and structured the participatory process without compromising its open character. The initial explorative workshops pushed them into being comfortable without having absolute control and clarity over the outcome of the project or the emerging discussions. At the same time, those workshops revealed the need for structuring elements such as the Future Workshop, which supported the project by providing a focus on a concrete outcome in the collaboration with the participants, as well as in the communication with the exhibition group.

We have shown how museum professionals implement participatory methods in their practice of audience collaboration and how they make dialogues work. We have illustrated how they reflect about the purpose of dialogues and how they co-produce knowledge with their participant groups, and how they adjust practices of designing visitor activities and exhibitions to hold the complexity of including other voices. The outcome of the PD process, the sound installation, was a more abstract invitation to visitor engagement with ethnicity, belonging and identity and was a result of museum professionals understanding how young people from multi-ethnic backgrounds think, engage and live with the topic. In this way, the PD process gave museum professionals insights that they would not have gained with more traditional audience involvement methods.

Acknowledgements

We would like to thank Groruddalen Ungdomsråd for their generous engagement in connecting us to the group of young people who participated in this project. Also a special thanks to Intercultural Museum in Oslo, who hosted one of the workshops arranged during the process.

References

Arnstein, S. R. (1969) 'A ladder of citizen participation', *Journal of the American Institute of Planners*, 35(4), pp. 216–224.
Bakhtin, M. (1981) *The dialogic imagination: Four essays*. Austin and London: University of Texas Press.
Bennett, T. (2006) 'Exhibition, difference and the "logic of culture"', in Karp, I., Kratz, C. A., Szwaja, L. and Ybarra-Frausto, T. (eds.), *Museum frictions: Public culture/global transformations*. Durham and London: Duke University Press, pp. 46–69.
Björgvinsson, E., Ehn, P. and Hillgren, P. A. (2012) 'Agonistic participatory design: Working with marginalised social movements', *CoDesign: International Journal of CoCreation in Design and the Arts*, 8(2–3), pp. 127–144.
Black, G. (2010) 'Embedding civil engagement in museums', *Museum Management and Curatorship*, 25(2), pp. 129–146.
Bourdieu, P. (2000) *Pascalian meditations*. Stanford, CA: Stanford University Press.

Participation and dialogue 81

Bourdieu, P. and Wacquant, L. (1992) *An invitation to reflexive sociology*. Chicago and London: The University of Chicago Press.

Dantec, C. A. L. and DiSalvo, C. (2013) 'Infrastructuring and the formation of publics in participatory design', *Social Studies of Science*, 43(2), pp. 241–264.

Dewey, J. (2007/1934) *Art as experience*. New York: Penguin.

Dindler, C. and Iversen, O. S. (2014) 'Relational expertise in participatory design', *Proceedings of the 13th participatory design conference: Research papers-volume 1*. New York: ACM, pp. 41–50.

Dysthe, O., Bernhardt, N. and Esbjørn, L. (2013) *Dialogue-based teaching: The art museum as a learning space*. Bergen: Fagbokforlaget.

Ehn, P. (2008) 'Participation in design things', in *Proceedings of the tenth anniversary conference on participatory design 2008*. New York: ACM, pp. 92–101.

Freire, P. (1970) *Pedagogy of the oppressed*. New York: Continuum.

Galani, A. and Moschovi, A. (2013) 'Other people's stories: Bringing public-generated photography into the contemporary art museum', *Museum and Society*, 11(2), pp. 172–184.

Graham, H. C. (2016) 'The "co" in co-production: Museums, community participation and science and technology studies', *Science Museum Group Journal*, 5(5).

Graham, H. C., Mason, R. and Nayling, N. (2013) 'The personal is still political: Museums, participation and copyright', *Museum and Society*, 11(2), pp. 105–112.

Hillgren, P. A., Seravalli, A. and Emilson, A. (2011) 'Prototyping and infrastructuring in design for social innovation', *CoDesign*, 7(3–4), pp. 169–183.

Holdgaard, N. and Klastrup, L. (2014) 'Between control and creativity: Challenging co-creation and social media use in a museum context', *Digital Creativity*, 25(3), pp. 190–202.

Krippendorff, K. (1995) 'Redesigning design: An invitation to a responsible future', in Tahkokallio, P. and Vihma, S. (eds.), *Design: Pleasure or responsibility*. Helsinki: University of Art and Design, pp. 138–162.

Latour, B. (2005) *Reassembling the social: An introduction to actor-network-theory*. Oxford: Oxford University press.

Laursen, D., Kristiansen, E. and Drotner, K. (2016) 'The museum foyer as a transformative space of communication', *Nordisk Museologi*, 1, pp. 69–88.

Light, A. and Akama, Y. (2012) 'The human touch: Participatory practice and the role of facilitation in designing with communities', *Proceedings of the 12th participatory design conference: Research Papers-volume 1*, ACM, pp. 61–70.

Linell, P. (2009) *Rethinking language, mind, and world dialogically*. Charlotte: Information Age Publishing.

Lynch, B. T. (2011) *Whose cake is it anyway?: A collaborative investigation into engagement and participation in 12 museums and galleries in the UK*. London: Paul Hamlyn Foundation.

Lynch, B. T. and Alberti, S. J. (2010) 'Legacies of prejudice: Racism, co-production and radical trust in the museum', *Museum Management and Curatorship*, 25(1), pp. 13–35.

Marstine, J. (2012) *The Routledge companion to museum ethics: Redefining ethics for the twenty-first century museum*. Oxon: Routledge.

Marttila, S. and Botero, A. (2013) 'The "openness turn" in co-design'. From usability, sociability and designability towards openness', in Smeds, R. and Irrmann, O. (eds.), *Co-create 2013: The boundary-crossing conference on co-design in innovation*. Espoo: Aalto University, pp. 99–111.

Message, K. (2006) *New museums and the making of culture*. Oxford: Berg.

Messenbrink, T. (2018) *The sound of folk – Participatory design of a sound-driven museum installation*, Master thesis. Department of Informatics, University of Oslo.

Meyer, M. (2010) 'Caring for weak ties: The natural history museum as a place of encounter between amateur and professional science', *Sociological Research Online*, 15(2), pp. 1–14.

Morse, N., Macpherson, M. and Robinson, S. (2013) 'Developing dialogue in co-produced exhibitions: Between rhetoric, intentions and realities', *Museum Management and Curatorship*, 28(1), pp. 91–106.

Mygind, L., Hällman, A. K. and Bentsen, P. (2015) 'Bridging gaps between intentions and realities: A review of participatory exhibition development in museums', *Museum Management and Curatorship*, 30(2), pp. 117–137.

Nelson, H. G. and Stolterman, E. (2003) *The design way: Intentional change in an unpredictable world*. Englewood Cliffs, NJ: Educational Technology.

Parry, R. (2007) *Recoding the museum: Digital heritage and the technologies of change*. Oxon: Routledge.

Phillips, R. B. (2003) 'Introduction', in Peers, L. and Brown, A. K. (eds.), *Museums and source communities: A Routledge reader*. London: Routledge, pp. 155–170.

Pihkala, S. (2018) *Touchable matters: Reconfiguring the practices of sustainable change through response-able engagements*, Doctoral dissertation. Faculty of Education, University of Oulu.

Saad-Sulonen, J., Eriksson, E., Halskov, K., Karasti, H. and Vines, J. (2018) 'Unfolding participation over time: Temporal lenses in participatory design', *CoDesign*, 14(1), pp. 4–16.

Sandell, R. (2016) *Museums, moralities and human rights*. Oxon: Routledge.

Schön, D. A. (1987) *Educating the reflective practitioner*. San Francisco: Jossey-Bass.

Smith, R. C. and Iversen, O. S. (2014) 'Participatory heritage innovation: Designing dialogic sites of engagement', *Digital Creativity*, 25(3), pp. 255–268.

Star, S. L. and Griesemer, J. R. (1989) 'Institutional ecology, translations' and boundary objects: Amateurs and professionals in Berkeley's Museum of Vertebrate Zoology, 1907–39', *Social Studies of Science*, 19(3), pp. 387–420.

Stuedahl, D. (2004) *Forhandlinger og overtalelser. Kunnskapsbygging på tvers av kunnskapstradisjoner i brukermedvirkende design av ny IKT* [*Negotiatons and Persuasions. Knowlegebuilding crossing knowledgetraditions in participatory design of new ICT*], Doctorate thesis. Department of Education, University of Oslo.

Stuedahl, D. and Skåtun, T. (2018) 'Collaborative design and museum media innovation. The "to and from the youth"– project: Including youth as experts', in Vestergaard, V. and Stuedahl, D. (eds.), *Media innovations and design in cultural institutions*. Göteborg: Nordicom, pp. 15–33.

Stuedahl, D. and Smørdal, O. (2015) 'Matters of becoming, experimental zones for making museums public with social media', *CoDesign*, 11(3–4), pp. 193–207.

Suchman, L. (2002) 'Located accountabilities in technology production', *Scandinavian Journal of Information Systems*, 14(2), pp. 91–105.

Taxén, G. (2004) 'Introducing participatory design in museums', *Proceedings of the eighth conference on participatory design: Artful integration: Interweaving media, materials and practices – volume 1*. New York: ACM, pp. 204–213.

Treimo, H. (forthcoming 2019) 'Sketches for a methodology on exhibition research', in Bjerregaard, P. (ed.), *Exhibitions as research*. London: Routledge.

Tzibazi, V. (2013) 'Participatory action research with young people in museums', *Museum Management and Curatorship*, 28(2), pp. 153–171.

Vidal, R. V. V. (2005) *The future workshop: Democratic problem solving*. Technical Report. Kongens Lyngby: Technical University of Denmark, DTU, pp. 1–22.

Weber, R. (2003) 'The reflexive researcher', *MIS Quarterly*, pp. v–xiv.

Artefact vignette #2: *The New Europe* app

Annelie Berner, Monika Halina Seyfried, Gabi Arrigoni and Areti Galani

1 Participants record their answers on the Passport, which visualises the inputs as partially filled rings depending on their answer.

2 Depending on their answers, different audio clips will play that put their answers into different contexts (political and social).

The New Europe app was designed to be a metaphorical passport that would evolve throughout a visitor's path in a pop-up living lab in the multi-ethnic neighbourhood of Nørrebro in Copenhagen. The app's interactive journey follows a path through a custom pavilion, where participants collaborate to create an alternative, fluid and dynamic statement about their collective identity and perspective on European values for the future. *The New Europe* app explores the potential of interactive data visualisation to emphasise the ambiguous, layered and changeable nature of identity. Further, it generates opportunities for dialogic exchange using the visualisation itself as a prompt for comparing one's own perspectives with a constellation of other ones. The first room of the pop-up living lab was conceived as an immersive threshold-space through distortions of lights and projections that suggest the reflexive nature of identity. The second room introduced third party voices into the process of identity 'rebuilding'. Here participants could listen to statements culled from current affairs or historical documentaries and related to the *Europe in 12 Lessons* pamphlet (European Commission 2011). The journey concludes with a sociable but also reflective space furnished with a group hammock where participants can look at the visualisation of their identity 'fingerprint', resulting from the interactions with all rooms in the living lab, alongside those of other living lab guests.

The progressive and relational articulation of the composite gradients visualising the participants' approach to European identity corresponds to the process of renewing or re-making cultural identity and one's own sense of belonging, calling into question fixed categories and embracing complexity and mobility. By doing so, *The New Europe* offers an immersive and data-driven take on topics frequently addressed in museums dealing with European history, such as migration, difficult coexistence and the significance of transnational or cosmopolitan cultural frameworks. Rather than following the predominant model of staging mediated encounters among visitors and members of different cultures, in *The New Europe*, people can also take a contemplative distance from their own usual self and come to see themselves as 'the other'.

The context of *The New Europe* app: www.cohere-4.com/living-lab/

Acknowledgements

The New Europe app was created through a collaboration between researchers in the Copenhagen Institute of Interaction Design (CIID) and Media, Culture, Heritage at Newcastle University, UK. We would like to thank all our colleagues who supported this process. Our thanks go to Matt Nish-Lapidus for creative technology. This research was carried out as part of the project CoHERE (2016–2019), which has received funding from the European Union Horizon 2020 programme under grant agreement NO 693289.

5   1215 in 280 characters

Talking about *Magna Carta* on Twitter

David Farrell-Banks

Introduction

Magna Carta is the defining legal document in British history. A respect for, and knowledge of, *Magna Carta* is an integral part of what it is to be British. So goes a stereotypical view of the influence that *Magna Carta* has on British life and identity today. For example, prospective new UK citizens are encouraged to 'find out: what does *Magna Carta* mean?' (Wales, 2013, p. 42). In the build-up to the United Kingdom (UK) European Union (EU) membership referendum in 2016,[1] references to *Magna Carta* began appearing regularly within political discourse. Prior to this, the UK Independence Party (UKIP), the foremost anti-EU party in the United Kingdom, pinned their 2015 General Election manifesto to references to the 800th anniversary of *Magna Carta*, with Nigel Farage,[2] then leader of UKIP, stating:

> If you believe in these things and that in this year, the 800th anniversary of Magna Carta, you believe we should seize the opportunity for real change in our politics; rebalance power from large corporations and big government institutions and put it back into the hands of the people of this country, then there really is only one choice.
>
> (UKIP, 2015, p. 3)

That choice being to vote for UKIP and, in the years following, to vote for the UK's exit from the EU. In the lead-up to the UK-EU referendum, a range of news articles replicated this discourse. For example, in the left-leaning broadsheet *The Guardian* (13 July 2016): 'Wetherspoon [UK pub chain] chairman Tim Martin says Brexit is a "modern Magna Carta"', and in the right-wing tabloid, *Daily Express* (30 May 2016): 'EU superstate laws strip Britain of its Magna Carta rights, writes [Conservative MP and leading Brexit campaigner] Jacob Rees-Mogg'. The impending departure of the UK from the EU, at least at the time of writing, is a testament to the success of this rhetoric.

In this chapter, I interrogate the meaning communicated in discursive uses of *Magna Carta*. I look in particular at such discourse on Twitter, a space which has become a fertile ground for political content. I make use of this content to discuss Twitter as a space where the potential for dialogic encounters, for example, through actions such as commenting or retweeting, are created. By moving away from traditional understandings of dialogue as one-to-one encounters (see Kent, 2013), instead understanding dialogue as the full range of human communication (Theunissen and Wan Noordin, 2012), as also discussed by Galani *et al.* in this volume (Chapter 2), this dialogic potential emerges. This discussion of the use of *Magna Carta* in online discourse is juxtaposed with its presentation at heritage sites to provoke discussion around the political position of such museums and heritage sites.

In the following sections, I discuss the current political context, most pertinently the continuing rise of right-wing populism in Europe and the United States. A brief history of *Magna Carta* follows, in addition to a discussion of the role of collective memory and ambiguous histories in the formation of collective identity. Subsequently, the analysis makes use of a selection of 10,562 tweets collected in June 2018. A selection of these tweets is analysed following the discourse-historical approach (DHA) to critical discourse analysis (CDA) proposed primarily by Ruth Wodak (Reisigl and Wodak, 2009; Wodak, 2015). The emergence of an internationalised nationalist discourse, within which the use of heritage is a key component, is discussed and the role of heritage sites in this context is questioned.

Populism and the political context

Right-wing populism (RWP) has been a feature of European politics since the end of the Second World War (Wodak and KhosraviNik, 2013, p. xvii). Populism does not offer 'a coherent ideology' but instead 'a mixed bag of beliefs [and] attitudes' (Wodak and KhosraviNik, 2013, p. xvii). At its heart is the concept of politics acting for *the people*, although the makeup of that group is left unarticulated (Pelinka, 2013, p. 3), alongside an anti-elitist or anti-establishment theme (Pelinka, 2013, p. 7). As these traits suggest, populism is not inherently right-wing. However, the brand of populism that I focus on here is notably right-wing in that its rhetoric is based upon the notion of *the people* as sharing ethnic, national or religious commonalities that are pitched against a converse *other*.

The success of this populist rhetoric can be seen across Europe, with the 2014 European Parliament elections bringing a significant rise in the number of RWP Members of the European Parliament (MEPs), from 38 in 2009 to 129 in 2014 (Wodak, 2015, p. 30). This trend has been mirrored in recent national elections, including in the relative successes of RWP parties such as the Freiheitliche Partei Österreichs (Freedom Party of Austria) in Austria, Alternativ für Deutschland (Alterative for Germany) and Lega in Italy. In the United Kingdom, whilst UKIP won only a single seat in the 2015 general election, the strength of their influence can be seen in policies adopted by the Conservative Party. In the years prior to the general election, then Prime Minister David Cameron was accused of adopting the 'prejudiced' politics of UKIP in an attempt to win back voters (Watt, 2013). Cameron's announcement in January 2013 of a commitment to a UK-EU referendum has been said to have had 'notably similar imagery' to a speech from UKIP leader Nigel Farage later that year (Cap, 2017, p. 71). The strength of influence from UKIP shows how the Brexit vote cannot be separated from the rise of RWP across Europe (Taylor, 2017, p. 73).

Whilst the Brexit campaign was often played out in a nationalistic manner, with a territorial member/non-member dichotomy as a central feature, common populist tropes and stylistic choices emerged within this. Whilst nationalism is often discursively constructed on territorial boundaries (the in/out membership of a nation), populism discursively constructs a notion of 'the people' as 'a powerless group through opposition to "the elite"' (De Cleen and Stavrakakis, 2017, p. 310). On a European level, RWP has also been recently characterised by 'opposition to immigration [and] concern for the protection of national [. . .] culture' alongside critiques of the EU and globalisation (Kaya, 2018, p. 3).

These populist tropes were a key feature of the Leave campaign during the UK-EU referendum. On 3 June 2016, three weeks prior to the referendum, Michael Gove – a Conservative cabinet minister at the time and one of the leading campaigners for the official Vote Leave campaign – told Sky News host Faisal Islam that people in the United Kingdom have 'had enough of experts' (Sky News, 2016). More tellingly, Gove later accused Mr Islam of being 'on the side of the elites', with Gove 'on the side of the people' (Sky News, 2016).

From the point in 2013 where a referendum was announced, we also see the use of references to moments in British history as a means of arguing for a leave vote. Specifically, we begin to see references to *Magna Carta*. This first emerges in Farage's speech to the UKIP conference in September 2013 where he states that 'Britain is different.' It has 'roots [which] go back seven, eight, nine hundred years with the Common Law. Civil Rights. Habeas Corpus. The presumption of innocence. The right to trial by jury. On the continent – confession is the mother of all evidence' (Farage, 2013). Although he doesn't point to *Magna Carta* explicitly, he does refer to themes commonly linked to this document – most clearly the right to trial. He also draws upon that populist trope of placing a national group against a foreign other. Britain has the right to trial – in the foreign continent, all it takes is a confession. Why might these references be so potent? And why is *Magna Carta*, in particular, evoked?

Magna Carta

When first issued in 1215, *Magna Carta* (meaning Great Charter) was a charter of necessity (Garnett, 2015). From 1213 to 1215, King John saw his grip on power recede, challenged by a group of rebel barons. In 1215, with his power almost lost, John met the rebel barons at Runnymede, near London – the location of the Magna Carta Memorial discussed later in this chapter – to present a 'charter of liberties' (Garnett, 2015) that would take some powers away from the King and return them to the barons.[3] The all-powerful rule of the King was removed, to be kept in check by rule of law (Warren, 1997, p. 239). As Holt (1992, p. 1) declares, this document was a failure and no more than three months after its sealing, civil war broke out. Despite this, the document was reissued in 1216, 1217 and 1225, before entering into statute with a final reissuing in 1297. Since then, 'in nearly all ages', those 'who knew little and cared less about the contents of the charter' have drawn upon it (Warren, 1997, p. 240). For Warren, this longevity comes not from the contents of the charter but from a perception of what it *meant*. This strength of meaning is increased by the lack of a written constitution in the United Kingdom, leaving *Magna Carta* to act as a proxy foundational constitution.

Notably, *Magna Carta* became associated with the assurance that no person could rule by will but must follow established law.[4] In addition, the misinterpretation of sections of the document in the seventeenth century led to the conflation of *Magna Carta* with the right to trial by a jury of one's peers (Warren, 1997, p. 240). These perceptions led to a perceived meaning of *Magna Carta* that is separate from its specific contents. It means a right to justice for all and the equal application of the law. A reference to *Magna Carta* is not a reference to the specific legalities contained within the document, but rather a more general reference to equality under law. This generality aids in allowing *Magna Carta* to be called upon in the present and given relevance to current political debate. In calling upon historical moments in this fashion, individual and collective memory is mobilised.

Memory and belonging

Ricœur (1990, p. 96) defines the 'historical event' as 'what actually happened in the past' whilst simultaneously recognising that such a complete understanding of the past is an impossible goal, as history continues to be reshaped in the present. This movement of history, where certain elements of the past resurface in new contexts, leads to a view of history not as linear, but rather as multilayered and complex (Koselleck, 1985), impossible to pin down or define (Wagner-Pacifici, 2010). Therefore, I do not discuss the historical *event* here but rather the historical *moment*, understood here as a representation of the past that is ambiguous, changing and moving. Our conception of a historical moment is not set in stone but constructed from the fragments that survive in written histories and heritage sites. This ambiguity allows for the reinterpretation of history to suit present needs, much as Warren suggests took place with *Magna Carta* in the seventeenth century. This ambiguity does not, however, negate the power of the past on the present. Rather, it enhances it.

These pasts emerge in the present in the form of mnemonic representations. It is memory, as Pierre Nora (1992) suggests, that plucks 'moments of history [...] out of the flow of history', before returning them, 'no longer quite alive but not yet entirely dead' (p. 7). More than that, memory is constantly changing across time as the cultures within which memories form change (Huyssen, 1995, p. 2). Our perceptions of what we remember will best fit our current conceptions of the world around us, reshaping the past events to make sense in the present. Memory and history share an ambiguity and subjectivity (Macdonald, 2013, pp. 13–14) that lend them to use in political discourse. The ambiguity of the past in historical representations, and in our mnemonic experience of it, allows for the reuse of the past in a manner which cannot be called a manipulation of fact, as the facts themselves are often blurry, but rather a (re)directing of the past towards a desired meaning.

This is important when we consider the role that memory and history play in the construction of collective identity. Influenced by Nora, although critical of his stark divide between history and memory, a range of scholars (Erll, 2011; Olick, 2007; Assmann, 2008) have detailed the connection between memory and the construction of collective identity. As Said (2000) states, representations of memory 'touch very significantly on questions of identity, of nationalism, of power and authority' (p. 176). In his notion of banal nationalism, Billig (1995) recognises that national identity is often reasserted through seemingly mundane symbols or actions. These symbols and actions are effective as they mobilise individual and collective memory (Paasi, 2016). Guibernau (2013) takes influence from Billig to construct a compelling account of the importance of a sense of belonging to any collective identity, suggesting that national identity provides a powerful sense of belonging. For Guibernau, national identity is constructed from five elements: the psychological (a feeling of belonging to a group, against a common enemy), historical (the selective use of history to build a collective memory, a connection to a lineage of ancestors), cultural (the recognition of symbols, rituals, and imagery), territorial (shared spaces that provide a good life to citizens), and political (a sense of common values).

Here, Guibernau demonstrates the power of both history and memory. A historic moment, and its ambiguity, can be used to create a collective memory that gives a historical sense of belonging, which in turn builds a sense of nationhood. This chapter argues that *Magna Carta* is mobilised and re-imagined in the (digitally extended) public sphere in a manner which allows it to work upon each of the dimensions of identity signalled by Guibernau. It is a piece of history used to create a sense of collective identity (historical). It is used to create belonging and closeness (psychological); the phrase itself has become a symbol (cultural); it is perceived to relate to shared political values (political); and it is used to create a sense of Britain as being stronger as an independent nation (territorial).

Methodology

The focal point of this chapter is a dataset of 10,562 tweets gathered between the 8th and 25th of June 2018. This period covered both the perceived anniversary of the first issuing of *Magna Carta* (15th June) and the second anniversary of the UK-EU referendum (23rd June). This period was chosen as a means of covering both a historical anniversary that we might expect to spark dialogue around *Magna Carta* as a piece of heritage, and an instance where it may be expected that there would be a spike in the political debate. The tweets have been gathered using the open source statistical computing programming language R (see Marwick, 2013; Bonacchi, Altawee and Krzyzanska, 2018). This provides real-time access to Twitter's filter (the operating system through which Twitter's search function operates), for the collection of data.[5]

The text of selected tweets is analysed using methods taken from critical discourse analysis. Here, I most closely follow the discourse-historical approach (DHA) (Wodak, 2015; Reisigl and Wodak, 2009). This entails giving equal focus to both the broader thematic contents of a text, and the specific detail, such as genre and arguments constructed (Wodak, 2015, pp. 50–51). Specific features of Twitter as a platform and genre are also considered (see KhosraviNik and Unger, 2016), including the anonymity and privacy allowed by the platform, the structural format of the posts, and the interaction facilitated by the platform. These methodologies are used as a means of identifying the ideologies contained within, and purposes of, each piece of text. The potential for these tweets to be considered dialogic encounters is discussed.

Whilst Twitter content is predominantly public (and all content analysed here is public as it is captured by the base Twitter search function), the level to which this is recognised to be public by a user might vary – Twitter users may each have a different concept of their 'imagined audience' (Marwick and boyd [sic], 2010, p. 115), the people who the user imagines will see their content. In this research, individual Twitter user names, which could be used to uncover the users' identities, are not included unless the content has been produced by a public figure. Public figures are taken to be individuals with a 'blue tick'[6] Twitter account, or individuals who self-identify within their profile as engaging in public discourse beyond Twitter. This acknowledges that the reproduction of public content may have long-term implications for the maintenance of anonymity (Page et al., 2014, p. 64).

Finally, the discussion includes reference to the display of *Magna Carta* at two heritage sites – Salisbury Cathedral and the Magna Carta Memorial at Runnymede. These sites were visited in June 2018, and represent two prominent, but notably different, heritage sites in the UK with links to *Magna Carta*. Salisbury Cathedral hosts a display of one of the few surviving original 1215 issues of *Magna Carta*. The memorial at Runnymede, conversely, is a relatively recent construction, intended to mark the area where the first issue of *Magna Carta* was produced. Whilst the landscape at Runnymede now includes a display designed to mark the 800th anniversary of *Magna Carta*'s first issue, I focus here upon the original memorial constructed on behalf of the American Bar Association. The data collected at these sites have been gathered following a critical museum studies approach (see Lindauer, 2006; Moser, 2010). Detailed field notes were taken regarding the sites, their setting and context, in addition to information regarding individual displays and objects. Each site was systematically photographed. These field notes and photographs form the basis of the discussion of heritage site representations of *Magna Carta* later. Aspects of the DHA also influenced the approach taken to the analysis of heritage sites, most notably in my discussion of a possible interpretation of features of the *Magna Carta* display at Salisbury.

Alternative uses of *Magna Carta*: Twitter and the heritage site

How does the interpretation of *Magna Carta* at heritage sites compare to its use by right-wing populist (RWP) groups? In the following section, I suggest that the central messages being projected when we see *Magna Carta* used by RWP groups may also be present in *possible readings*, but by no means the only reading, of 'official' narratives presented at such sites (see Mason, 2004). As such, I do not seek to suggest that these interpretations themselves intentionally adopt, or indeed sanction, an RWP position. Rather, through illustrating the appropriation of such historical moments for the propagation of divisive viewpoints, I suggest that we can better understand their use by RWPs and, therefore, more effectively counter the positions they are used to articulate. I further suggest that Twitter is a space with significant dialogic potential. By understanding such digital platforms as a place of public dialogue, we can better engage with public understandings and uses of histories such as *Magna Carta*.

Magna Carta on Twitter

KhosraviNik and Unger (2016) draw attention to the changing relationship between producers and consumers of media facilitated by social media. Where previously there has been one-way interaction between the producers of media and consumers, social media allows for the emergence of a digital media *produser* (Bruns, 2006): those who both produce and use social media content. This suggests that traditional power structures may be broken down. Previously, this feature of social media saw it considered a powerful democratising tool, a 'liberation technology' (Diamond, 2010). However, it is clear that power imbalances remain prevalent on such platforms, expressed on Twitter in the imbalance between the number of followers and the number of followed (Marwick and boyd *[sic]*, 2010, p. 117). For example, the leader of the UK Labour Party, Jeremy Corbyn, has 1.85 million followers at the time of writing, but follows just 2,500 himself. The England footballer Harry Kane has 2.38 million followers, but follows only 239. These figures may have millions of individuals paying attention to the content that they produce, but that attention is not returned. These imbalances show that Twitter is as unequally structured as the non-digital public sphere, with some users having the potential to exert significantly greater influence.

The data gathered here similarly suggest that social media retains the power to elevate certain voices above others. For example, over two-thirds of the tweets captured receive ten or fewer retweets (the *verbatim* sharing of a post). The fact that the average retweet count (48) is higher than this shows us that this data are skewed by a minority of tweets that receive high levels of interaction. A small number of posts garner most of the interaction. Many of these posts, as is shown in later examples, come from individuals in positions of public influence. Recognising these imbalances of influence, I focus this analysis upon tweets that have gained most interaction in terms of retweets, and therefore have been shared most widely on Twitter. Whilst other forms of interaction are possible (such as commenting on or liking a tweet), here I use retweet counts as the most significant indicator of the reach of a post.

In these power imbalances, the apparent dialogic limitations of Twitter emerge. If a requirement of dialogue is to create a two-way 'personal encounter' (Gutierrez-Garcia, Recalde and Pinera-Camacho, 2015, p. 745), then Twitter, it would seem, does not fulfil that requirement. Indeed, some have recently gone so far as to suggest such technology is endangering democracy through the proliferation of misinformation and 'hyperpartisan' political commentary (Tucker et al., 2018, p. 3). However, as I discuss later, through expanding our conception of dialogue, we can see the breadth of dialogic encounters taking place through Twitter. I, therefore, suggest that, whilst power imbalances remain present on Twitter, the platform does act as a space with dialogic potential.

In these data,[7] the most extensive interaction is found among users/account holders with traditionally public political roles. Additionally, two of the most prominent political tweets both relate not to British politics, but to issues in the United States and Canada. First, from the former White House ethics lawyer and political commentator Richard Painter:

> Tweet 1 [3,716 Retweets (RTs)]: 'The President can't obstruct justice because he is the top law enforcement officer. The President can't have a conflict of interest. Like a king before Magna Carta the President IS the law. And congress is too busy with its own corruption to care'.

And second, from Lisa Raitt, deputy leader of the opposition in Canada:

> Tweet 2 [603 RTs]: 'Fantastic point of order by @AndrewScheer. He reminded the House that today in history the Magna Carta was signed giving people fundamental rights and privileges. The King could no longer impose taxes without approval of the ppl. We deserve to know the cost of the carbon tax'.

In each instance, *Magna Carta* is used as a means of calling attention to an abuse of power, a denial of justice and 'rights' of the people. In the first instance, Painter equates President Trump to a King ruling above law. By talking of Congress's 'own corruption', he tacitly suggests that Trump is himself engaged in corrupt activity. In the second instance, our attention is drawn to the opposition leader in Canada, Andrew Scheer, and his use of *Magna Carta* to suggest that the incumbent government is hiding details of taxation from its citizens. Like King John, it suggests a government unjustly taxing people against their rights. The nuance of the political context in each instance is lost, given over to a punchy statement that fits the Twitter character limit. What remains is a call for justice and fairness.

Wodak (2015, pp. 52–53) suggests various *topoi* (discursive thematic tools), both formal and content related, that are common to right-wing populist (RWP) rhetoric, each of which has an associated argumentation scheme. For example, in the *topos of threat*, an argument would suggest that because of a certain threat or danger, a particular action or actions are necessary. In this instance, I suggest that we see the emergence of the *topos of justice*. This is discourse that focuses upon issues of justice, freedom and individual rights. Here, the argument formulates as follows: if there is a denial of justice, or individual rights, then actions must seek to return such justice. In Tweet 2, this works as follows: because you are being unfairly/ unjustly taxed, you should act by supporting the opposition party.

Equally important here is the emergence of *Magna Carta* as a transnational discursive tool. It plays a role not just in the collective memory of those in the UK but is considered equally to have discursive strength across the Atlantic. This is a trait recognised by RWPs, and borne out by their use of *Magna Carta* on Twitter. Take the following two posts, one of which is the most retweeted post captured within these data:

> Tweet 3 [986 RTs]: 'Britgov to citizens: We will shut you up and lock you up if you don't like how we are dealing with a plague of child sexual abuse. We will shred every document of freedom from the Magna Carta to the UN Declaration on Human Rights to protect our privileges'. [This post links to a news article regarding the arrest of British right-wing activist Tommy Robinson].[8]
>
> Tweet 4 [3,928 RTs]: 'From the Magna Carta to this. How far our cousins across the pond have fallen. #FreeTommyRobinson'. [Alongside a photo of Tommy Robinson's arrest].

The argumentation scheme in both instances is again one of the denial of justice by those in power. The perspective put forward is that the British government may as well 'shred' *Magna Carta* as we have returned to a time of injustice. Notably, both of these tweets have been posted by users based in the United States. Much as the mainstream political commentators see value in reference to *Magna Carta*, so the RWPs follow suit. Through reference to Tommy Robinson and *Magna Carta*, a discourse is created by the RWPs where the United Kingdom, the birthplace of *Magna Carta* and, therefore, the birthplace of fairness and justice, is under threat. According to RWPs, this is threatened by those in power, who – it is claimed – ignore the rights of citizens. By making use of the arrest of Tommy Robinson, this abuse of power is tacitly linked by RWPs to the issue of immigration, particularly from predominantly Muslim countries, as this has been the focal point of Robinson's political ire.

This argumentation scheme is again present in the following post from Ezra Levant, co-founder of the Canadian right-wing news and political commentary website Rebel Media:

> Tweet 5 [481 RTs]: 'A final thought. When I first visited Tommy, I was excited to be in the UK, a land I associated with Shakepeare *[sic]*, Churchill, Magna Carta, etc. I soon learned that Britain is gone; it's in a museum. I am disillusioned. And the cheering from the left confirms I am not wrong'.

The series of posts within which this is contained include references to UK prisons 'dominated by Muslim gangs' and the need to separate 'mosque and state'. He praises Robinson for speaking up for the 'forgotten people'. These posts return to common populist tropes – the creation of an in-group, the undefined 'people', and the positioning of this group against common enemies, in this case predominantly Muslims, and the elite in the form of incumbent governments.

In these posts from RWPs, the *topos of justice* becomes more specific. In the first two examples discussed earlier, the narrative could be directed towards a wide range of people. Anyone who supports the opposition party in Canada, or who disagrees with Trump in the USA, could be a target of this discourse. In the case of the RWPs, the argument applies only to a particular group of 'citizens', 'cousins' or 'people'. It is a *topos of justice for those who belong*. The DHA method gives focus to 'positive self- and negative other-presentations' (Wodak, 2015, p. 52), a feature present here. *Magna Carta* means justice for those who are legitimately British, or at least white and Western. According to the earlier tweets, this is being endangered by the outsider group – the non-white, frequently Muslim, populace. The ambiguity of the historical moment allows for *Magna Carta* to become a potent tool within these arguments. The detail of what *Magna Carta* means, its legal application and relevance today, are subsumed by the vague notion of its standing as a bastion for fairness and justice, for the giving of power to 'the people'. Here, the limits of Twitter, the necessity of short statements giving little room for nuance, emerge. Such limitations have led to Twitter being characterised as a space of dissonance and antagonistic public discourse (Pfetsch, 2018). However, I contend that the platform retains the potential to be a space where dialogic encounters take place as demonstrated in the following section.

The dialogic potential of Twitter

As discussed, there is often an imbalance in Twitter interactions that would suggest that it is a place of monologue rather than dialogue, particularly if we are to frame dialogue as purely a 'one-on-one relational tool' (Kent, 2013, p. 341), or as always necessitating a face-to-face interaction. Kent (2013, p. 339) goes so far as to state that the expansion of digital technology, and the related movement of political action to online spaces, has resulted in politics becoming 'a private activity'. However, the 'uncritical' assumption that dialogue must mean 'two-way symmetrical communication' has been accused of failing to recognise the complexity of human communication (Theunissen and Wan Noordin, 2012). Such complex communication can include dialogic encounters that are asynchronous and asymmetrical, no longer face-to-face, such as those which emerge on Twitter.

First, consider the role of the 'reply' function on Twitter – the space in which users can publicly comment on any post. Tweet 4 from earlier, which focuses upon the trial of Tommy Robinson, has received 428 replies at the time of writing. These responses range from supportive ('Disgraceful!') to the critical ('Mr Robinson . . . was interfering in a criminal case', see Figure 5.1). Additionally, the Twitter platform will allow replies to any of these individual comments, meaning there are instances where a series of comments between two or more individuals may emerge (Figure 5.1).

This dialogue is often asynchronous – the encounter in Figure 5.1 takes place over three days. Despite this, a dialogue between them emerges, if we understand dialogue as a communication process that can also be asynchronous and asymmetrical as discussed earlier. This is one aspect of the dialogic *potential* of Twitter. Whilst the original producer of the content does not, in any of the five instances presented, respond themselves, the tweets can create a space within which dialogue can emerge in a relatively traditional, person-to-person manner.

The dialogic role of the retweet should also be considered. Whilst a one-to-one conversation might not be taking place, an asymmetrical form of dialogue may emerge. If we view dialogue as 'a process and not an outcome' where 'opportunities for expression should be created' (Theunissen and Wan Noordin, 2012, p. 10), then Twitter is a potentially powerful dialogic tool. Through the act of retweeting, individuals repeat these posts often (though by no means always) as an act of public agreement. Bayerl and Stoynov (2014) suggest that the process of sharing or adapting memes can shape public dialogue through acting as expressions of a political stance. Similarly, the act of retweeting could influence ongoing public dialogue by giving certain viewpoints greater presence within this extended public sphere. Whilst this is not an act of one-to-one dialogue, it influences ongoing dialogic processes by raising certain voices above others, giving certain statements a greater presence in this political space.

However, the scope of such dialogue can be limited. Whilst conversations such as that in Figure 5.1 do appear, they are outnumbered by instances of the simpler act of retweeting. In other words, whilst constructive dialogue

Figure 5.1 A conversation between two individuals in the 'reply' thread to Tweet 4.
Note: The conversation takes place across three days, from the 28th to the 30th of May.

is present, it is of much less prominence than the space given to the reproduction and dissemination of a specific statement. Whilst this does have dialogic features, these are potentially weak as the power remains weighted towards the arguments within the original statements.

In the use of *Magna Carta* seen in these data, the most prominent statements are those that build arguments around the aforementioned *topos of justice*. The power of this type of argument is clearer when noting that this rhetoric can be linked to Guibernau's five elements of national identity. It is the use of *Magna Carta* as an evocative piece of national history (historical), which projects a symbolic power in its communication of the right to freedom and justice (cultural), a symbol which in turn relates to the suggested shared political values of genuine UK citizens (political). Through its use to link to a narrative of the superiority of a particular in-group, the sense of belonging for those who consider themselves to be part of this group is encouraged (psychological). Finally, in presenting the UK and USA as superior, as places of such freedoms, the strength and power of these nations is reasserted (territorial). This is a trait that appears to be recognised by right-wing populist (RWPs) through its use on Twitter and other media channels. *Magna Carta* takes on a role as an international tool for nationalistic dialogue. It is a statement that calls for greater recognition of rights for certain populations, certain groups who belong. It gives the RWP groups a historical legitimacy that might be understood to add weight to their arguments.

Heritage sites and *Magna Carta*

The transnationalism of *Magna Carta* is also evident at heritage sites. Nowhere is this more apparent than in the site of the Magna Carta Memorial at Runnymede. The original part of this heritage site is the 'American Bar Association Memorial to Magna Carta'. Constructed in 1957, this memorial, the first structure at Runnymede to mark the first issuing of *Magna Carta*, states that it is 'to commemorate Magna Carta, symbol of freedom under law' (see Figure 5.2).

The landscape at Runnymede is further tied to American history and heritage by the presence of a memorial to John F. Kennedy set into the same landscape, on land gifted to the USA by the United Kingdom for this purpose. This site, a memorial to an apparently defining piece of British heritage, is dominated by links to the USA. This is itself a reflection of the foundational influence that *Magna Carta* is said to have had on American politics (see Warren, 1997). The memorial also acts to assert the continued relevance of Magna Carta currently. A number of inscriptions note the return of delegates from the American Bar Association on five occasions since the memorial's construction, most recently in 2015, on each occasion asserting the continued importance of upholding the principles of *Magna Carta*. The site creates a narrative similar to that in the first two Twitter posts discussed earlier (Tweets 1 and 2): through the commemoration of *Magna Carta*, the American Bar Association, and the politicians who have taken part in ceremonies at the site, recognise individual rights and freedoms, *ergo* they can be trusted.

Similarly, the 'past-presencing' (Macdonald, 2013) of *Magna Carta*, that is, the manner with which it is given relevance in the present through acts of individual and/or collective remembering, is not limited to political discourse. At Salisbury Cathedral, home to one of the few surviving original copies of *Magna Carta*, the exhibition that houses *Magna Carta*

Figure 5.2 The Magna Carta Memorial at Runneymede, erected by the American Bar Association.
Source: Photo: David Farrell-Banks.

repeatedly asks visitors what relevance *Magna Carta* has to the visitor today. It pulls *Magna Carta* into the present and relates it to a range of prevailing issues. This exhibition also explicitly seeks to reassert *Magna Carta*'s relevance on a global level. Images of protest movements in Egypt and an interactive display showing levels of corruption, freedom of press and commitment to the *United Nations Declaration of Human Rights* across the world are used to show that 'the struggle for social justice is an ongoing one'. Whilst the intention here may be to demonstrate the importance of struggles for justice on a global level, the exhibition presents only such struggles outside of the West. Britain emerges in the exhibition as the birthplace of civil liberties, some of which are still not granted elsewhere. It has the potential to push the notion of Britain as a place of absolute freedom and justice, with other nations, most frequently outside Europe, as places of continuing oppression.

For those inclined towards right-wing populist (RWP) viewpoints, such as those present in the aforementioned Twitter posts, this narrative may be appropriated to contend that Britain must act to protect freedoms against an influx of immigration from Middle Eastern countries where those liberties, present here since *Magna Carta* was first sealed in 1215, are still not recognised. However inadvertently, this exhibition could convey a message that can fit with the *topos of justice* as used by RWPs earlier. The UK is the home of *Magna Carta*, and therefore the home of significant freedoms, a place for a positive self-presentation, against the negative other-presentation of foreign nations who do not follow the example set by the UK.

Through platforms such as Twitter, we have access to a range of discourses regarding history and heritage that may have previously remained hidden, or] spoken only in private settings. Rather than moving political dialogue into private spaces, Twitter can make what was once private public. This analysis has shown a prevalence on Twitter of the rhetorical use of *Magna Carta* by RWPs as a means of encouraging nationalistic and RWP ideals. Whilst I do not by any means suggest that heritage sites share the ideals espoused within these posts, it is the case that certain narratives – of Western superiority as leaders in justice and freedom – are readily appropriated and expanded upon by RWPs to give credibility to their own political agenda. By building upon content present in 'official' settings, these appropriations of history are given potency due to the role that museums and heritage sites play in influencing public conceptions of national collective identity.

Museums have been conceptualised as institutions which have the power to be enlisted by governments to not only inform but also discipline a populace, in a Foucauldian sense. Bennett argued this case in relation to nineteenth-century museums in some European cultures like the United Kingdom (Bennett, 1995). He argued that museums had such power that they could act, alongside other institutions such as schools or prisons, as tools for ruling elites to 'discipline' individuals towards acting in concordance with those elites' vision of society. Additionally, Macdonald (2013) suggests that museums are integral in the creation of the imagined sense of belonging to a nation state, which is key to a sense of national identity (Anderson, 1983). In each of these instances, there is a recognition of the role that museums, and histories, play in influencing the collective identity of the wider society in which they exist.

At Salisbury and Runnymede, the importance of *Magna Carta* to a sense of British (or even American) national identity is articulated. The continuing relevance of *Magna Carta*, particularly to a British and American public, is asserted in the objects on display and their interpretation. It is done in such a way that can allow for the UK or the USA to be positioned as upholders of liberty and freedom, and the recognition of this is reconfirmed as a part of the collective identity of these nations. These aspects of *Magna Carta* are reflected in the manner in which it is talked about online. Whether a heritage site, or its staff, considers itself to be consciously political or not, historic moments – particularly those which, like *Magna Carta*, have a position in a national collective memory – will often appear in political dialogue and discourse. Some of that political discourse, such as that expressed online, can now be accessed and viewed through digital platforms such as Twitter, giving us access to conversations and viewpoints that may previously have remained private. The ways in which people talk about these histories, far beyond the boundaries of the heritage site itself, can be seen by heritage professionals.

That knowledge of the discursive use of historic moments such as *Magna Carta* can be used to create more reflexive and responsive representations of the past within the 'official' narratives presented at heritage sites. Through giving attention to the use of moments such as *Magna Carta* on platforms such as Twitter, in other words by 'listening' to the discourse and dialogue produced on Twitter, staff at sites of 'official' representations of these histories can increase their awareness of the political use of the pasts they present. Whilst I do not suggest that this should encourage such sites to engage directly with the type of Twitter discourse shown earlier, it can encourage a more reflexive approach to the representations produced at heritage sites themselves. It could encourage these sites to produce content where such divisive uses of the past are countered more actively within their own interpretations of the histories they represent.

Conclusion

At a time when 'fake news' has become a common phrase, it may be tempting for us to assume that right-wing populist (RWP) groups misrepresent history for their own means. I have suggested within this chapter, however, that the discourses that make use of history most potently, do so in a manner which shows similarity to the official, heritage site representation of these historic moments. The central meaning contained within the discursive use of *Magna Carta*, that of fairness and justice under law, is similar across these different spaces. The way in which *Magna Carta* is used, and the range of topics with which it is linked, suggests a wide-reaching recognition of, if not necessarily a deeper interest in, the role that history continues to play in our lives. *Magna Carta* is brought into political discourse not only as a distant piece of history, but also as something that has significant relevance to actions today. Through digital spaces such as Twitter, we have a new level of access to this discourse and its use within dialogic encounters on such platforms. The form of dialogue may have changed, but a powerful sense of the political role of the past remains.

These pasts are appropriated by RWPs through social media to further the politics of division that they espouse. This chapter has suggested that these RWPs seek to give added credibility to these political stances by appropriating and adding their own political spin to narratives present at 'official' heritage sites, particularly regarding the superiority of the UK (and the USA). This can act as a challenge to heritage sites to give greater attention to the manner in which the histories they present are used politically. In doing so, the interpretation produced at these sites could more reflexively counter divisive uses of the past.

Acknowledgements

This research was supported by a Research Excellence Academy doctoral studentship from Newcastle University, UK.

Notes

1 This referendum, on 23 June 2016, asked UK citizens whether they wished to remain a member of the EU, or to leave. 51.9% of voters opted to leave. At the time of writing, the negotiations to leave continue.
2 Nigel Farage was one of the most prominent figures pushing for a leave vote in the UK-EU referendum. See Kelsey (2015) for more detail.
3 A full translation of the 1215 *Magna Carta* is available at: www.bl.uk/magna-carta/articles/magna-carta-english-translation (Accessed: 2 November 2018). For a discussion of Magna Carta in a European context, see Reynolds (2016).
4 A concise discussion of the relevance of *Magna Carta* today is available at: www.bl.uk/magna-carta/articles/magna-carta-in-the-modern-age (Accessed: 2 November 2018).
5 The code used was based on that found at http://politicaldatascience.blogspot.com/2015/12/rtutorial-using-r-to-harvest-twitter.html (Accessed: 13 August 2018).
6 This refers to the presence of a blue tick on a Twitter profile used to confirm that the account is genuine. This suggests that the individual is in the public eye enough to be at risk of imitation.
7 These data has been gathered over a limited period, and therefore does not capture long-term trends associated with 'Magna Carta' on Twitter that may be shown by a larger project operating with big data.
8 Tommy Robinson, a prominent far-right figure in the UK, was arrested for live streaming a 'news report' outside the trial of individuals accused of sexual abuse. Reporting during trial is often illegal in the UK and can result in a mistrial.

Bibliography

Anderson, B. (1983) *Imagined communities: Reflections on the origin and spread of nationalism*. London: Verso.
Assmann, J. (2008) 'Communicative and cultural memory', in Erll, A., Nunning, A. and Young, S. (eds.), *Cultural memory studies: An international and interdisciplinary handbook*. Berlin: Walter de Gruyter, pp. 109–118.
Bayerl, P. S. and Stoynov, L. (2014) 'Revenge by photoshop: Memefying police acts in the public dialogue about injustice', *New Media and Society*, 18(6), pp. 1006–1026.
Bennett, T. (1995) *The birth of the museum: History, theory, politics*. London: Routledge.
Billig, M. (1995) *Banal nationalism*. London: Sage.
Bonacchi, C., Altawee, M. and Krzyzanska, M. (2018) 'The heritage of Brexit: Roles of the past in the construction of political identities through social media', *Journal of Social Archaeology*, 18(2), pp. 174–192.
Bruns, A. (2006) 'Towards produsage: Futures for user-led content production', in Sudweeks, F., Hrachovec, H. and Ess, C. (eds.), *Proceedings: Cultural attitudes towards communication and technology 2006*, Perth: Murdoch University, pp. 275–284.
Cap, P. (2017) *The language of fear: Communicating threat in public discourse*. London: Palgrave Macmillan.
De Cleen, B. and Stavrakakis, Y. (2017) 'Distinctions and articulations: A discourse theoretical framework for the study of populism and nationalism', *Javost – The Public*, 24(4), pp. 301–319.
Diamond, L. (2010) 'Liberation technology', *Journal of Democracy*, 21(3), pp. 69–83.
Erll, A. (2011) *Memory in culture*. New York: Palgrave Macmillan.
Farage, N. (2013) *Speech to the UKIP party conference*. Available at: https://blogs.spectator.co.uk/2013/09/nigel-farages-speech-full-text-and-audio/ (Accessed: 7 January 2018).
Garnett, G. (2015) 'Magna carta through eight centuries', in *Oxford dictionary of national biography*. (Online only). Oxford: Oxford University Press.
Guibernau, M. (2013) *Belonging: Solidarity and division in modern societies*. Cambridge: Polity Press.
Gutierrez-Garcia, E., Recalde, M. and Pinera-Camacho, A. (2015) 'Reinventing the wheel? A comparative overview of the concept of dialogue', *Public Relations Review*, 41, pp. 744–753.
Holt, J. C. (1992) *Magna carta*. Cambridge: Cambridge University Press.
Huyssen, A. (1995) *Twilight memories: Marking time in a culture of amnesia*. New York: Routledge.
Kaya, A. (2018) 'Right-wing populism and islamophobism in Europe and their impact on Turkey – EU relations', *Turkish Studies*.
Kelsey, D. (2015) 'Hero mythology and right-wing populism: A discourse-mythological case study of Nigel Farage in the mail online', *Journalism Studies*, 17(8), pp. 971–988.
Kent, M. L. (2013) 'Using social media dialogically: Public relations role in reviving democracy', *Public Relations Review*, 39, pp. 337–345.

KhosraviNik, M. and Unger, J. W. (2016) 'Critical discourse studies and social media: Power, resistance and critique in changing media ecologies', in Wodak, R. and Meyer, M. (eds.), *Methods of critical discourse studies*. London: Sage, pp. 205–233.
Koselleck, R. (1985) *Futures past: On the semantics of historical time*. Cambridge, MA: MIT Press.
Lindauer, M. (2006) 'The critical museum visitor', in Marstine, J. (ed.), *New museum theory and practice: An introduction*. Malden: Blackwell, pp. 203–225.
Macdonald, S. (2013) *Memorylands: Heritage and identity in Europe today*. London: Routledge.
Marwick, A. E. and boyd, d. (2011) 'I tweet honestly, I tweet passionately: Twitter users, context collapse, and the imagined audience', *New Media and Society*, 13(1), pp. 114–133.
Marwick, B. (2013) 'Discovery of emergent issues and controversies in anthropology using text mining, topic modeling, and social network analysis of microblog content', in Zhao, Y. and Cen, Y. (eds.), *Data mining applications with r*. Amsterdam: Elsevier, pp. 63–93.
Mason, R. (2004) 'Museums, galleries and heritage: Sites of meaning-making and communication', in Corsane, G. (ed.), *Heritage, museums and galleries: An introductory reader*. Oxon: Routledge, pp. 221–237.
Moser, S. (2010) 'The devil is in the detail: Museum displays and the creation of knowledge', *Museum Anthropology*, 33(1), pp. 22–32.
Nora, P. (1992) *Realms of memory volume 1*. Columbia: Columbia University Press.
Olick, J. K. (2007) *The politics of regret*. New York: Routledge.
Paasi, A. (2016) 'Dancing on the graves: Independence, hot/banal nationalism and the mobilization of memory', *Political Geography*, 54, pp. 21–31.
Page, R., Barton, D., Unger, J. W. and Zappavigna, M. (2014) *Researching language and social media: A student guide*. Oxon: Routledge.
Pelinka, A. (2013) 'Right-wing populism: Concept and typology', in Wodak, R., KhosraviNik, M. and Mral, B. (eds.), *Right-wing populism in Europe: Politics and discourse*. London: Bloomsbury, pp. 3–22.
Pfetsch, B. (2018) 'Dissonant and disconnected public spheres as challenge for political communication research', *Javnost: The Public*, 25(1–2), pp. 59–65.
Reisigl, M. and Wodak, R. (2009) 'The discourse-historical approach (DHA)', in Wodak, R. and Meyer, M. (eds.), *Methods for critical discourse analysis*. London: Sage, pp. 87–121.
Reynolds, S. (2016) 'Magna carta in its European context', *History*, 101(348), pp. 659–670.
Ricœur, P. (1990) *Time and narrative Vol. 1*. Chicago: Chicago University Press.
Said, E. W. (2000) 'Invention, memory, and place', *Critical Inquiry*, 26(2), pp. 175–192.
Sky News. (2016) *Michael Gove – 'EU: In or out?'*. Available at: www.youtube.com/watch?v=t8D8AoC-5i8 (Accessed: 30 August 2018).
Taylor, G. (2017) *Understanding Brexit: Why Britain voted to leave the European Union*. Bingley: Emerald Publishing Limited.
Theunissen, P. and Wan Noordin, W. N. (2012) 'Revisiting the concept "dialogue" in public relations', *Public Relations Review*, 38, pp. 5–13.

Tucker, J. A., Guess, A., Barbera, P., Vaccari, C., Sigel, A., Sanovich, S., Stukal, D. and Nyhan, B. (2018) *Social media, political polarization, and political disinformation: A review of the scientific literature*. Menlo Park: Hewlett Foundation.

UKIP. (2015) *Believe in Britain: UKIP manifesto 2015*. Newton Abbott: UKIP.

Wagner-Pacifici, R. (2010) 'Theorizing the restlessness of events', *American Journal of Sociology*, 115(5), pp. 1351–1386.

Wales, J. (2013) *Life in the United Kingdom: Official study guide*. Norwich: The Stationary Office.

Warren, W. L. (1997) *King John*. New Haven: Yale University Press.

Watt, N. (2013) 'David Cameron "must stop pandering to UKIP prejudices"', *The Guardian*. Available at: www.theguardian.com/politics/2013/dec/27/cameron-stop-pander-ukip-immigration (Accessed: 30 August 2018).

Wodak, R. (2015) *The politics of fear: What right-wing populist discourses mean*. London: Sage.

Wodak, R. and KhosraviNik, M. (2013) 'Dynamics of discourse and politics in right-wing populism in Europe and beyond: An introduction', in Wodak, R., KhosraviNik, M. and Mral, B. (eds.), *Right-wing populism in Europe: Politics and discourse*. London: Bloomsbury, pp. xvii–xxviii.

Artefact vignette #3: *Erdi*

Annelie Berner, Monika Halina Seyfried, Gabi Arrigoni and Areti Galani

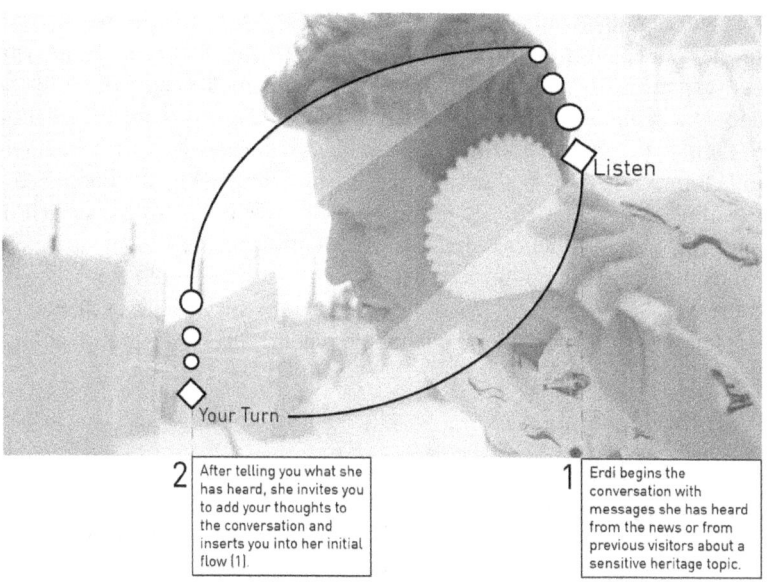

2 — After telling you what she has heard, she invites you to add your thoughts to the conversation and inserts you into her initial flow (1).

1 — Erdi begins the conversation with messages she has heard from the news or from previous visitors about a sensitive heritage topic.

Erdi is the way the computer pronounces R.D., which abbreviates the title 'Reflective Devices'. As the full name indicates, it is designed to engage participants to reflect upon a given topic. Furthermore, it does not simply gather reflections: it stores, structures and reorganises them such that it becomes the facilitator of an asynchronous dialogue among her conversation partners.

Erdi elaborates on key elements of a dialogic experience starting from its fundamental prerequisite of readiness to listen to other people's perspectives and feeling safe and comfortable. Differently to many museum dialogic exhibits that pose a question to visitors and record their answers, *Erdi* prompts her interlocutors to first engage with other people's statements or opinions and pieces of knowledge, sourced from Twitter, books, speeches and so forth. Having set the expectations for the dialogue, *Erdi* invites her conversation partners to contribute their thoughts, simply asking, 'And what do you think?' At this point, *Erdi* listens for input, and if she hears nothing, she will shift back to sharing other thoughts she has heard elsewhere.

Erdi's user interface is relatively blank and unfamiliar, while still referencing 1950s telephones that separate input and output; the users listen in one cone and speak in another. Furthermore, *Erdi* consists essentially of an audio experience, following initial testing that demonstrated how voices elicited a stronger and more intimate engagement than written messages. A faceless and interface-less device, *Erdi* critically addresses some of the typical features of today's communication practices on social media, such as anonymity, lurking, filter bubbles and asynchronicity, as well as the location of digital platforms within the public sphere. At the very least, *Erdi* attempts to facilitate reflection before speaking, as she simply will not record or 'listen' if users have not already been through her first steps of the asynchronous dialogue – which require listening to other people's thoughts before recording your own opinions. It experiments, therefore, with the notion of 'purposeful listening' as a feature of a democratic society and exchange.

The context of *Erdi*: www.cohere-4.com/home/2017/8/21/prototype-iii

Acknowledgements

Erdi was created through a collaboration between researchers in the Copenhagen Institute of Interaction Design (CIID) and Media, Culture, Heritage at Newcastle University, UK. Our thanks go to Karina Jensen for design and creative technology. This research was carried out as part of the project CoHERE (2016–2019), which has received funding from the European Union Horizon 2020 programme under grant agreement NO 693289.

6 Dialogues and heritages in the digital public sphere

Areti Galani, Rhiannon Mason and Bethany Rex

The chapters in this volume have suggested that the term 'dialogue' often raises normative expectations related to its potential as a vehicle for positive change. As Nicholas Burbules (2000), one of the leading theorists in dialogic approaches to education, proclaims in the opening section of his analysis of the limits of dialogue as a critical pedagogy:

> It seems that hardly anyone has a bad word to say against dialogue. A broad range of political orientations hold out the aim of 'fostering dialogue' as a potential resolution to social conflict and as a basis for rational public deliberation.
>
> (p. 251)

This also holds true for the fields of heritage and museum studies and practice since the 1990s, as well as in the European policies concerned with intercultural dialogue, as outlined in this volume. Rodney Harrison (2012) similarly provides strong support for this sentiment when he argues for dialogicality to be seen as an inherent aspect of the conceptualisation of heritage. Through the lens of a 'dialogical model', he argues, heritage 'is seen as emerging from the relationship between people, objects, places and practices' (p. 4). In this context, the concepts of *materiality, connectivity* and *dialogue* are 'central to understanding the role of heritage in contemporary societies' (ibid.) and allow us to deal more productively with uncertainty, crisis and controversy through the adoption of 'hybrid forums' in decision-making. Given such promise attributed to dialogues and dialogicality, this volume is a timely and critical intervention which has examined and tested the potential of both.

The case studies found in Chapters 3, 4 and 5 of this volume have provided insights into how the dialogical potential of heritage, and particularly ideas connected with European heritage as a common or shared assembly of values, expressions and materialities, is perceived, practised and mobilised within the context of digital culture. These experiences of 'lived' heritage-dialogicality were framed at the outset through the lens of current policies and documentation produced by the European Commission and the Council of Europe, especially flagship documents such as the *Faro Convention on the Value of Cultural Heritage for Society* (Council of Europe, 2005), the *White Paper on Intercultural Dialogue – Living Together As Equals in Dignity* (Council of Europe, 2008), and the *Recommendation of the Committee of Ministers to member States on the Internet of citizens* (2016) among others. Responses to both the policy and the case studies were found in three 'artefact vignettes', which aimed to showcase how a research-through-design methodology can allow us to experiment with some of the challenges emerging for European heritage and dialogue in digital culture.

These interdisciplinary and multimodal ways of approaching the topic of this volume have made evident that quite different conceptualisations and applications of the idea of dialogue can be identified in contemporary museum and heritage practice and thinking, as these enter the digital public sphere. While we do not seek to provide a definitive account of how dialogue, and the specific notion of intercultural dialogue, are mobilised and practised in current thinking, we are able to identify a preliminary set of observations to guide future thinking on this topic. These epistemological reflections, in turn, lead us to articulate three areas where further intervention is required to enable digital heritage practice to become dialogue oriented. These relate to methods for dialogue, skills, policies and strategies that reflect the tripartite relationship between European heritage, dialogue and digital culture.

Epistemological reflections

An overview of both the literature and practice outlined in the contributions in this volume makes apparent that one of the most fundamental factors is whether dialogue is understood as a useful end in, and of, itself *or* as useful only when it leads to action. This underpins the articulation of a distinction between two approaches: (a) dialogue-as-purpose and (b) dialogue-as-purposive. This distinction is a useful initial step to help us reflect on the often-assumed qualities of dialogic discourse as well as to articulate two productive ways in which cultural institutions support dialogue, emerging through the chapters of this volumes: (a) by creating opportunities for *dialogue as reflexive action*, and (b) by supporting *dialogue as purposeful listening*. It is these four elements that we discuss in the following sections.

Dialogue-as-purpose

In this way of thinking about dialogue, the end goal is to create the conditions for *dialogue to take place*, with little interest in the outcome of this

Dialogues, heritages in the digital sphere 111

interaction. The dialogue may be construed quite simply as the act of 'talking face-to-face' with someone. It may be specified as talking with 'others' with whom one may not interact in everyday life, away from the museum. It may also mean dialogue with the 'other' through interpretative strategies, that is, bringing people in museum and heritage settings into contact with the 'other' but via the intermediary device of the exhibition rather than directly (as discussed by Arrigoni and Galani in Chapter 3). In the latter situation, the visitor finds out or may even hear from the 'other' but at a distance, which does not require direct interaction. Alternatively, the encounter may take place online so that the 'other' can see what has been responded to but may not engage directly with its authors or their point of view (as seen in Chapter 5 by Farrell-Banks). The goal here then is that an exchange of some kind takes place (of information, of opinion, of views) but the end goal of this exchange is not prioritised or even particularly clearly defined.

Dialogue-as-purposive

By contrast, in this framing, *dialogue is the first step, the means, towards something else*, whether that be social change, political activism or outcomes relating to the museum's decision-making processes (such as collaborative decision-making, exhibition planning, and co-developing content for different audiences, as seen in Chapter 4 by Stuedahl *et al.*). Again, there are different types of dialogue in operation. Dialogue can be seen as part of the broader democratic goals of an institution and happens through participatory forms to provide a conceptual space where people can meet to figure out how to engage in representative democracy processes and systems. Dialogue here functions as a prompt and enabling mechanism to encourage and support contributors to dialogue to review and possibly change their position on contemporary issues, or how they might identify, or disidentify, with certain subject positions. As outlined in Chapter 4, dialogues of this kind are also iterative and evolve over a longer time frame.

We observe that the key difference between these two approaches to dialogue is how they are positioned in relation to change and transformation – and, ultimately, in relation to addressing cultural difference in Europe and the conflicts that embodies. In the former practices, we suggest, *change* is conceptualised as one of the *potential outcomes* of a reflexive encounter; in the latter practices, *change* becomes a *goal* that is pursued through a dialogic process. The boundaries between these practices are also blurred. For example, it is hard to clearly distinguish whether the dialogic process that took place in the *Science, Identity, and Belonging* project, discussed by Stuedahl *et al.* in Chapter 4, can be seen as an end in, and of, itself – that is, to create a welcoming space for members of the institution and members of a youth group to encounter each other and work together, or as a process that had as a specific goal to change both the institution's and the youths' attitudes towards each other in relation to who has the privilege to author cultural content. As the authors present, change in approaches and attitudes indeed took place. However, this was often gradual and unanticipated and required openness, reflexivity and reflection on behalf of all involved in the process. It also required physical and intellectual space where experimentation with the dialogic process was possible.

Moreover, the chapters in this volume suggest that although cultural institutions have experience in facilitating and/or instigating dialogue in their own premises, primarily within a participatory museological framework (Chapters 3 and 4), they are less confident with purposefully extending these practices into the digital public sphere. This comes through clearly in the interviews with museum professionals presented by Arrigoni and Galani in Chapter 3, in which interviewees expressed their dilemmas in encouraging (or not) participation on their institution's social media platforms in relation to the history of Jewish people and the Holocaust. Furthermore, Farrell-Banks's contribution (Chapter 5) demands that we both pay attention to the asynchronous dialogic encounters about heritage on Twitter, which often take place without the involvement of cultural institutions, and reflect on the limits of institutional involvement on dialogic encounters online in the context of right-wing politics.

Assumed qualities of discourse

As explored in Chapter 2, in relation to discussions about European identity, the literature about dialogue tends to be premised on the importance of a positive recognition, and respect for, difference and diversity, which is simultaneously framed within a call to acknowledge the unity of human experience as an overarching framework. This accords with the European Union's (EU) official motto of 'Unity in diversity', which came into use in 2000 and is meant to describe 'how Europeans have come together, in the form of the EU, to work for peace and prosperity, while at the same time being enriched by the continent's many different cultures, traditions and languages' (European Union, n.d.). Notably, policy makers and heritage practitioners alike tend to imagine dialogue resulting to consensus and civil engagement rather than discord. This is evident in European policy on intercultural dialogue in which dialogue is often aligned with terms such as 'respectful exchange' and 'mutual understanding' and antithetically positioned in relation to terms such 'mutual suspicion' and 'intolerance' (Council of Europe, 2008). Such approach to dialogue reinforces Stanley Deetz and Jennifer Simpson's (2004) observation that use of the word often 'foregrounds specific normative hopes' (p. 141) for society, with the

Dialogues, heritages in the digital sphere 113

conditions in which such dialogic interactions are perceived to take place often offering suggestive visions for the kind of societies that its advocates hope to achieve. These normative hopes for a culturally diverse but ultimately harmonious future is a common, often unproblematised, trope in many EU policies relating to either culture and heritage, intercultural dialogue or digital citizenship. They also underpin significant initiatives such as the 2018 official year of *European Cultural Heritage* and investment in infrastructure programmes, such as *Europeana*.

However, as already discussed in Chapter 2 of this volume, cultural difference and diversity are not fixed phenomena but as a socially constructed set of ideas and practices are fluid and in constant negotiation. The contributions to this volume evidence the potentialities of museum space to host and inspire such negotiation. In this context, what emerges is that cultural institutions are ideally positioned to advance dialogue in two aspects of practice: (a) in *creating dialogic opportunities for reflexive action*, and (b) in *supporting dialogue as purposeful listening* which, while clearly complementary, are not synonymous.

Dialogue as reflexive action

Dialogue as understood here involves a kind of reassessment of one's own position and a recognition of the situatedness of subjectivity – the place from where one speaks. This is also a position that Paulo Freire takes up in his work on education, where, he argues, 'dialogue cannot be reduced to the act of one person's "depositing" ideas in another, nor can it become a simple exchange of ideas to be "consumed" by the discussants' (Freire, 2005, p. 89). Rather, dialogue in the Freirean sense is, as Stuedahl *et al.* explore in their chapter, oriented towards a pragmatics of implementation that puts a primacy on authentic dialogue as both 'reflection and action' (ibid., 2005, p. 86) in which the subject, in particular, is responsible for this process.

While Freire's work focuses on dialogue that takes place among individuals, we see the value of this particular emphasis on reflexivity and action as potentially significant for heritage institutions in a networked society. Innocenti (2016), exploring the role of cultural institutions in issues of migration in Europe, argues that 'cultural networks and networking have played an increasingly important role as infrastructures for supporting transnational and cross-sectoral cooperation and cultural dialogue, and creating cultural value' (p. 277). Cultural networks, according to Innocenti (ibid.), can be 'instrumental' in the role of cultural institutions in Europe in addressing the 'need for a coherent narrative, a story of a society and its cultural, historical and social contexts' (p. 278). Equally, we argue, network society and the ongoing investment on digitisation schemes offer cultural institutions

114 *Areti Galani et al.*

a unique opportunity to overcome the limitations of their often historically determined narratives and spheres of knowledge by connecting them to those of their communities and other institutions. The promise of connectivity through and around heritage resources among individuals, institutions and groups not only affords cultural institutions the opportunities to contribute to their own awareness of their socio-cultural world but also provides these institutions with tools to create spaces (actual and online) for *reflexive*, that is, relational and situated, identity construction and dialogue. Attempts of this kind were reflected upon by the interviewees in Chapter 3 of this volume; these, however, also pointed at the challenges these attempts to connectivity between institutions and other communities face in the context of the public sphere, as discussed later.

Dialogue as purposeful listening

Complementarily to the notion of dialogue as reflexive action, the chapters of this volume also highlighted the conceptualisation of dialogue as civic listening (especially Chapter 3). In this conceptualisation, it is the act of active listening and being heard that matters, rather than a need to convert another to one's own viewpoint and resolve or cede all differences of opinion. Wood, for example, writes:

> [D]ialogue does not necessarily idealize or seek common ground. The search for (and belief in) common ground may thwart, rather than facilitate, genuine dialogue, because almost inevitably the dominant culture defines what ground is common or legitimate. Rather than the reproductive goal of finding 'common ground' or 'resolving differences,' dialogue allows differences to exist without trying to resolve, overcome, synthesize, or otherwise tame them [. . .]. By extension, this means that dialogue does not necessarily preclude standing one's ground firmly, but it does require that in doing so one remains open to the call of the other.
>
> (Wood, 2004, p. xviii)

In the context of many current societies where public discourses are highly polarised around specific contentious topics such as migration, national identity and religious beliefs, this idea of 'purposeful listening' or 'civic listening' appears to be extremely relevant (see Chapter 3). This idea assumes that the right to speak is contingent on the obligation to listen; reciprocity is key. One qualification here is that although this kind of purposeful listening does not require anyone to give up their position, it presumes that participants in dialogue accept conflict as a potentially useful and productive position. This requires a conceptual transformation of a kind. It means that heritage institutions should adopt exhibitionary and engagement methods that allow them not only to display controversy but also to explore conflict and, specifically, to model behaviours which encourage the public to engage in purposeful listening and encounters with other opinions in a way that does not lead to a simple breakdown of communication. In other words, we recommend that part of future institutional practice around digitally mediated dialogues needs to involve the development of a pedagogy of purposeful listening and of engaging with differences of opinion that can be shared with audiences.

The limitations of dialogue

While it is possible to see the productive potential of the conceptualisations of dialogue outlined earlier, there are some obvious limitations in thinking through how this would work in practice. Wood was writing about the value of not pushing for consensus of opinion in 2004 before the global release of Facebook and before the mass co-option of social media for political persuasion and propaganda, particularly by right-wing interests. As discussed in Chapter 2, there is a range of opinions, some optimistic and some deeply pessimistic, about the likelihood of people encountering and responding positively to views other than their own given that today's online environment is increasingly dominated by user preference learning algorithms which tailor our online experiences to match our pre-existing interests and values. As Papacharissi (2002) pointed out in the early 2000s, reflecting on the promise of the Internet to revive the public sphere: '[t]he same anonymity and absence of face-to-face interaction that expands our freedom of expression online keeps us from assessing the impact and social value of our words' (p. 16). This is a significant factor in how we can now think about the potential for dialogue in the digital public sphere to bridge different worldviews. This might well lead us to be less hopeful about the likelihood for digital dialogues and self-reflection to take place without being supported and encouraged. However, it can also lead us to argue that the need to try to find ways for societies to develop better ways to have public conversations about difficult topics is an urgent task for all stakeholders. Similarly, we would argue that the importance of continuing to strive for a digital public sphere based on strong civic values and principles is greater now than ever before.

From another angle, this volume has pointed towards the commonly held perception of the role of public heritage institutions in Europe as representing the dominant, and often monologic, cultural *status quo*, through their collections and cultural resources that have a symbolic value in relation to narratives emerging from contested actions in Europe's past. These representations and articulations have framed and constrained interactions between diverse communities and between institution and individuals historically and, we argue, limit our collective capacity to engage in dialogue. Within the digital public sphere, which promises openness and plurality but 'does not guarantee democratic and *rational* discourse' (Papacharissi, 2002, italics added), the dilemma for public cultural institutions is whether they can open up for dialogue the topics and practices that underpin their own existence and popularity. We need to acknowledge, however, that institutions operate within cultural, political and economic contexts; these play a role in shaping institutional behaviours and boundaries as heritage organisations negotiate new ways of maintaining their practices while increasing their relative market power and value in the global scene, an aspiration articulated for public cultural institutions in national scale (e.g. the *Culture White Paper* [Department of Media Culture and Sport, 2006] in the UK) and European policies on access to digital cultural resources and digitisation. These institutions, we observe, are progressively caught in the competing demands, on one hand, of harnessing digital technology to increase their 'soft power' globally and, on the other hand, prioritising dialogic activities that promote a new kind of humanist digital civicness for them and their publics.

It is also important to acknowledge that the digital public sphere, as we refer to it in this volume, continues to reflect the point of view of individuals and institutions whose 'lived' experiences of digital culture takes place in democratic societies, with little appetite to officially regulate participation and access to digital cultural resources and platforms of expression. The debates and critiques of the dialogue-oriented practices by cultural institutions articulated in this volume should be seen in this context. We are mindful that many of the presumptions underpinning our discussions of dialogue and public discourses do not apply in countries where there is state control or censorship of the media and public sphere. The shape and nature of public conversations through digital media in those countries has already attracted significant scholarly attention but it is beyond the scope of our study here. We now turn to the brief discussion of three areas of future practice to which this volume contributes.

Ways forward

Through the engagement with the relevant policies and literatures, the *in-focus* explication of practices concerning dialogue and digital technologies (particularly through Chapters 3, 4 and 5) and the provocations proposed by the artefact vignettes, three areas of practice emerge as significant in contributing to a productive roadmap for European heritage and dialogue

Dialogues, heritages in the digital sphere 117

in digital cultures: *the role of design as a relational and future-oriented method*, alongside *the development of transmedial digital skills and literacies*, and *the articulation of strategies and policies of convergence between digital heritage and dialogue.*

Enabling dialogue through design

The role of design in museological practice was brought up in both Chapters 3 and 4 – in the former, Arrigoni and Galani referred to design in relation to the development of dialogic digital exhibits in both European and other international contexts; in the latter, Stuedahl *et al.*, specifically focused on the application of design approaches to engender dialogic interactions between museum staff and a group of youth of multi-ethnic background to co-create a digital interactive sound installation for the Norwegian Museum of Science and Technology. Farrell-Banks also alerted us to how design features of Twitter engender certain kinds of dialogic behaviours. Last, the artefact vignettes put forward alternative and future-oriented treatments of dialogue in digital cultures, re-examining, for example, the performativity of dialogic 'civic' listening (artefact vignette #3) and the use of visualisation as generative of reflexive thinking around identity. All these instances point towards the capacity of design and research-through-design methodologies to enable heritage professionals, researchers and policy makers to imagine both alternative forms of dialogue and alternative structures that may support productive engagements with alterity within both physical and digitally mediated museum spaces. On a practical level, we argue that design gives cultural institutions more readily the permission to use experimentation to co-create new meanings and forms of expression around heritage, which have the capacity to align with their audiences' (and non-audiences') everyday experiences, as demonstrated by Stuedahl *et al.* in chapter four and articulated by the ERICArts report (2008), discussed in previous chapters.

On a purposive level, we argue, design methods furnish the European cultural sector with a renewed ability to imagine, digitally. Wood, in her reflection on how dialogue can be engendered within asymmetric contexts of power, concludes: '[i]t is difficult to imagine what might motivate such efforts on the part of those who are comfortable within current social structures, but precisely this kind of imagining is needed' (Wood, 2004, p. xx). Work that is presented in this volume points to the capacity of design to deal with the unknown through imagination: 'the role of the unknown as a driver of meaning formation' becomes apparent 'when we put imagination on the "agenda" of design' (Folkmann, 2014, p. 8), as it becomes apparent in the 'futurescaping' workshop with heritage professionals, which was the context of the *Transformation Machine* (artefact vignette #1).

This is not to advocate that designing for dialogue in digital culture should be preoccupied specifically or primarily with the future. This volume is mindful of McPhail's (2004) comment in the context of interracial dialogue, that 'dialogue that is future-oriented runs the risk to side-step unacknowledged differences in the interlocutor's perspectives'. We instead advocate the role of design in enabling the European digital heritage sector to develop what Balsamo (2011) calls a 'technological imagination' – or what we have informally called in our discussions about this volume 'digital imagination' – that is, in the case of digitally mediated dialogues in heritage, the capacity of heritage professionals, community groups, individuals and policy makers to imagine dialogic relationships, spaces, structures and processes *with* digital technology and not *about, for* or *because of* it.

Developing techno-social literacy skills to enable dialogue

Undoubtedly, development of digital literacies is a significant step forward in cultivating both 'technological imagination' as discussed earlier and confidence among heritage professionals, individuals and communities in engaging with dialogue around heritage in the digital sphere. This urgency is fully represented in all relevant European Union policies, which see the development of digital literacy skills as a means to enhancement of creativity among Europeans and strengthening of democracy by reinforcing 'access to and participation in open culture' (Recommendation of the Committee of Ministers to Member States on the Internet of Citizens, 2016). This prioritisation of digital skills development as a means to inclusive cultural experiences also permeates the 2018 report on *Promoting Access to Culture via Digital Means: Policies and Strategies for Audience Development*, which suggests that digital technologies allow a 'fundamental disentangling of what used to be understood as mainstream and hard-to-reach groups' (p. 18) as digital literacies (or lack of) lead to re-configuration of groups with access to culture.

However, what is important to highlight here is that this development of digital skills and literacies should specifically and consciously aim to combine technical competencies with social/dialogic ones. As Chapter 2 specifically articulated, drawing on van Dijk's (2011) definition of network society, it is important to pay attention to the fact that in networked society, technical and social networks come together. Therefore, the skills required to support dialogue should also reflect this hybrid state; in other words, the 'convergences between different literacy traditions' identified by the recent *Recommendation of the Committee of Ministers to Member States on the Internet of Citizens* (Council of European Union, 2017) is the key for skills development to foster both institutions and individual 'consumers, creators

Dialogues, heritages in the digital sphere 119

and prosumers' (ibid.) of cultural resources who are also attuned to the dialogic (or lack of) dimensions of these practices. This leads us to the third aspect of this roadmap, the development of relevant policies and strategies.

Developing dialogue through policy and strategy

One of the key observations by several of the contributors to this volume is that although museums and heritage organisations are often engaged in hosting and supporting dialogue in their space, this is commonly initiated and delivered by specific departments, or even individuals, in the organisation, often within a consciously articulated participatory museological frame of practice (see Chapters 3 and 4). Conversely, overarching institutional strategies around dialogue are sparse despite the policy framework provided by the Council of Europe's (2008) *White Paper on Intercultural Dialogue*. This reflects, we propose, the slippage in the use of terms 'dialogue', 'intercultural dialogue' and 'dialogicality' in both heritage and policy discourse. On one hand, the inherent dialogicality of heritage renders strategies on dialogue in heritage institutions potentially redundant or, in the best case scenario, tautological to mission statements, exhibition strategies and programming. On the other hand, intercultural dialogue is treated as an instrument and is subsumed in strategies around community engagement and outreach. Although we do not advocate here the proliferation of institutional strategies on dialogue, we suggest that it is worth raising the question: if 'hardly anyone has a bad word to say against dialogue' as suggested earlier, what institutional strategies are better suited to promote the value of dialogue within an institutional framework and whose responsibility is it to reflect on and advance dialogic practices around heritage in heritage institutions?

We observe similar ambiguities in the strategies related to digitisation of heritage and access to digital heritage, which fall short of addressing the dialogic aspect and potential of this work. Chapter 2 has already highlighted that in European policy, the dialogic aspect is primarily dealt with through policy around interculturalism, heritage and diversity, whereas policies around digital heritage are primarily, but not solely, concerned with digitisation of cultural resources and broadening access to digital cultural production and consumption. It may be that this is the reason why individual heritage institutions and national level policies also do not make a strong enough connection between digital heritage and dialogue; that is, because the supranational policy and funding framework does not encourage them to do so. Although the emphasis of *A New European Agenda for Culture* (2018) on the interconnections between cultural heritage and digital is a positive step to this direction, we also advocate that strategies and initiatives across these two areas should also be specifically linked to activity around intercultural dialogue in Europe, rather than treating it as their outcome or their context. The starting point has to be that given there is this ever-growing and powerful digital public sphere, heritage organisations, community groups, politicians and policy makers need to develop *new principles and frameworks* for thinking through how the convergence between cultural heritage and digital developments will interface with the tensions and opportunities of dialogue, as articulated in Chapter 2. We argue that other media platforms such as television provide insights into how long-standing institutions in these domains have already worked through such issues. In this process, heritage organisations need to think specifically about what kind of digitally mediated dialogues around and through heritage are envisaged in this context, who will participate in them, what do they want to achieve from them and how can the breakdown of dialogue be avoided?

In the conclusion of her critical history of online social media platforms, the media theorist José van Dijck (2013) poetically suggests that '[t]he ecosystem of connective media needs watchful caretakers and diverse gardeners in order for it to be sustained' (p. 176). It is now time, we argue, for cultural institutions to re-imagine themselves as both caretakers and gardeners playing an active role in this new ecosystem; to mobilise the agency that is afforded to them by the digital and their long-standing experience in engaging with many forms of alterity in order to propose new and innovative ways of thinking and, as a result, transcultural being.

Acknowledgements

We would like to thank our colleague Dr Joanne Sayner, who provided feedback on earlier versions of this chapter. This research was carried out as part of the project CoHERE (2016–2019), which has received funding from the European Union Horizon 2020 programme under grant agreement NO 693289.

References

'A New European Agenda for Culture (2018) *European commission*. Available at:https://ec.europa.eu/culture/sites/culture/files/commission_communication_-_a_new_european_agenda_for_culture_2018.pdf (Accessed: 14 January 2019)

Balsamo, A. (2011) *Designing culture: The technological imagination at work*. Durham, NC: Duke University Press.

Burbules, C. N. (2000) 'The limits of dialogue as a critical pedagogy', in Trifonas, P. (ed.), *Revolutionary pedagogies*. New York: Routledge.

Dialogues, heritages in the digital sphere 121

Council of Europe. (2005) 'Council of Europe framework convention on the value of cultural heritage for society, Faro', *Council of Europe Treaty Series*, 199. Available at: www.coe.int/en/web/conventions/full-list/-/conventions/rms/0900001680083746 (Accessed: 7 January 2019).

Council of Europe. (2008) *White paper on intercultural dialogue: Living together as equals with dignity*. Strasbourg: Council of Europe.

Council of European Union. (2017) *Promoting access to culture via digital means: Policies and strategies for audience development*. Luxembourg: Publications Office of the European Union.

Deetz, S. and Simpson, J. (2004) 'Critical organisational dialogue: Open formation and the demand of "otherness"', in Anderson, R., Baxter, L. and Cissna, K. (eds.), *Dialogue: Theorizing difference in communication studies*. London: Sage Publications. pp. 141–158.

Department of Media, Culture and Sport. (2016) *Culture white paper*. Available at: www.gov.uk/government/publications/culture-white-paper (Accessed: 14 January 2019).

ERICArts. (2008) *Sharing diversity – National approaches to intercultural dialogue in Europe report*. Brussels: European Commission.

European Union. (n.d.) *About EU*. Available at: https://europa.eu/european-union/about-eu/symbols/motto_en (Accessed: 14 January 2019).

Folkmann, M. N (2014) 'Unknown positions of imagination in design', *Design Issues*, 30(4), pp. 6–19.

Freire, P. (2005) *Pedagogy of the oppressed*. London: Continuum.

Harrison, R. (2012) *Heritage: Critical approaches*. London: Routledge.

Innocenti, P. (2016) 'Cultural networks and social inclusion of migrants in Europe: Heritage, ICT, and participatory governance', *International Information & Library Review*, 48(4), pp. 274–286.

McPhail, M. L. (2004) 'Race and the (im)possibility of dialogue', in Anderson, R., Baxter, L. and Cissna, K. (eds.), *Dialogue: Theorizing difference in communication studies*. London: Sage Publications, pp. 209–224.

Papacharissi, Z. (2002) 'The virtual sphere: The internet as a public sphere', *New Media and Society*, 4(1), pp. 9–27.

'Recommendation of the Committee of Ministers to Member States on the Internet of Citizens CM/REC(2016)/2'. (2016) *Council of Europe*. Available at: https://search.coe.int/cm/Pages/result_details.aspx?ObjectId=09000016805c20f4 (Accessed: 14 January 2019).

van Dijck, J. (2013) *The culture of connectivity*. Oxford: Oxford University Press.

van Dijk, J.G.M. (2006) *The Network Society: Social aspects of new media*. 2nd edn. London: Sage.

Wood, J. (2004) 'Foreword – Entering into dialogue', in Anderson, R., Baxter, L. and Cissna, K. (eds.), *Dialogue: Theorizing difference in communication studies*. London: Sage Publications, pp. xv–xxiii.

Index

Note: Page numbers in italics indicate figures.

2005 UNESCO *Convention on the Protection and Promotion of the Diversity of Cultural Expressions* 13, 10

access as delivering dialogic ethos, cultural heritage 28
Adair, B., Filene, B. and Koloski, L. 3
Affleck, J. and Kvan, T. 21
Agustín, Ó. G. 19, 20
alterity 3; conceptualisation(s) of 18, 27; and dialogue 18–22; and otherness, conceptualisations of 12
Aman, R. 19
Anderson, B.: "imagined communities" 53
Anderson, R., Baxter, L. and Cissna, K. 15
appropriation 39–40; of Magna Carta (online), by right wing 26
Archive of the Migrant Memory (YouTube) 45
artefacts 68; Mudec, Museum of Cultures, Milan 45–46
Artefact vignette(s) 110, 116; *Erdi* 106–107; *The New Europe* app 84–85; *The Transformation Machine* 60–61
articulation: of dialogue 15; of digitalisation 27; of European heritage institutions as neutral 12; of European sense of belonging 38; of the self 30; of strategies and policies of convergence 117; of subjectivity 53
Ashley, S. 37
ASK (mobile app), Brooklyn Museum, dialogic interactions 41

asymmetry, patterns of access 17; of power 52
audiences and institutions, power inequality between, re–balancing of 39
"Authorised Heritage Discourse" (AHD) 14

Badenoch, A. 28
Bakhtin, M. M. 12, 15, 20, 28, 63
Balsamo, A. 118
Burbules, N. 109
Barrett, J. 37
BBC Trending 11
behaviour(s): civic 2; cultural 2
Bennett, T.: *The Birth of the Museum* 25; power of museums 101
Bhabba, H., dialogic space as "third space" 22
Bhambra, G. 19, 20
Billig, M., banal nationalism 90
Black, C. 62
Boast, R. 16
Bodo, S.: dialogic space as "third space" 22
Bodo, S., Gibbs, K. and Sani, M. 25
Bonacchi, C., Altawee, M. and Krzyzanska, M. 91
boundaries: cultural 2; geographical 2
"boundary encounter," *vs.* participatory processes 62
Bourdieu, P. 68
Bourdieu, P., and Wacquant, L. 68
Brexit 4, 86
broadcasting, digital 10

Calligaro, O. 19
Cameron, D. 37
Cameron, David, Prime Minister 88
Canadian Heritage Information
 Network (CHIN) 21
challenges, of making dialogues work 66
Chinatown History Museum 15
*Chinatown History Museum
 Experiment* 3
civic listening 39; *see also* listening
civicness, digital 29
Clifford, J.: "contact zone" 16–17
*Commission's Recommendation on the
 Digitisation and Online Accessibility
 of Cultural Material and Digital
 Preservation* 10
communication practices,
 networked 2
communities, as co–curators and
 co–creators, participatory design
 practices 40
community and dialogue, elision
 between 20
conceptualisation(s): of alterity 27; of
 dialogue 114; of digitally mediated
 dialogue 42
"contact zone": de–centralised
 network *vs.* museum/community
 paradigm 17; digital 51–52
convergence: of cultural heritage and
 digital developments, principles and
 frameworks for thinking about 119;
 strategies and policies, articulation
 of 117
Council of Europe 9, 10, 13, 14, 27,
 112, 119
Council of European Union 23, 25, 118
critical discourse analysis (CDA) 87
cultural: boundaries 2; "turn to
 openness" 62
cultural heritage: access as delivering
 dialogic ethos 28; defined 13–15;
 and digital developments, new
 principles and frameworks for
 thinking about convergence of 119
cultural institution(s), European 2
cultural networks, as instrumental
 in addressing need for coherent
 narrative 113
cultures, individuals and experience,
 intersection of 40

Culture White Paper, Department of
 Media Culture and Sport 116
curatorial reflexivity 62
curators, exhibition 51

Dahlberg, L. 24
Daily Express 87
database, participatory 53–54
De Cleen, B. and Stavrakakis, Y 88
Deetz, S., and Simpson, J. 15, 112
De Jong, S. 53
Delgado, E. 3, 22
design, European cultural sector, ability
 to imagine digitally 117
Dewey, J. 63
dialogic discourse: dialogue–as–
 purpose, creating the conditions
 for dialogue to take place 110–11;
 dialogue as purposeful listening
 109; dialogue–as purposive, first
 step towards something else 111;
 dialogue as reflexive action 109
dialogic focus 3
dialogic heritage practice(s), digitally
 mediated 4
"dialogic museum" 15–16, 39–40
dialogic practice(s): designing for 4;
 shifting perspectives as characteristic
 of, giving authority and legitimacy to
 participants 70
dialogic relationship, as continuous,
 reciprocal exchange 20
dialogue: articulation of 15;
 conceptualisation(s) of 114;
 limitations of 115; as "a key to
 Europe's future" 9; as process not
 outcome 97; as purposeful listening,
 importance of listening and being
 heard 109, 114; as reflexive action
 113; as tool for mediation, *vs.* natural
 part of societal interaction 20
dialogue and community, elision
 between 20
dialogue–as–purpose, creating the
 conditions for dialogue to take place
 110–11
dialogue–as purposive, as first step
 towards something else 111
dialogue as reflexive action:
 conceptualisation(s) of 114; dialogic
 discourse 109

dialogue–driven museum(s) 39
dialogue(s) 26; digitally enabled, limited consideration of by exhibition curators 51; digitally mediated 2; digitally mediated vs. direct human exchange 51; diversity in language around 2; as full range of human communication, vs. one-to-one encounters 87; as "a key to Europe's future" 9; as means of achieving democratic process 39; see also intercultural dialogue (ICD); Twitter
Diamond, L. 93
difference, as "form of connection" 20
digital, techno–deterministic approach to, by institutions and policy makers 16
Digital Agenda for Europe 10
digital broadcasting 10
digital civicness 29
digital contact zone 51–52
Digital Cultural Heritage policy 16
digital installation, The, *The Sound of Folk* 65
digital interfaces 44
digitalisation, articulation of 27
digital literacy, as means to safeguarding cultural diversity, overly future oriented 27
digitally enabled dialogue(s), limited consideration of by exhibition curators 51
digitally mediated, dialogue(s) 2, 51; conceptualisation(s) of 42
digital media 54
Digital Natives (exhibition), Aarhus Centre for Contemporary Art 40
digital platforms: and silencing of the other, vs. idea of infinite connectivity 24; technological limitations built in 26
digital practices 39
digitisation: as opportunity for institutions to connect with communities and other institutions 113–14; power dynamics of 28; reconceptualisation as process, vs. techniques and tools 28
discourse: museological 12; philosophical 12

discourse–historical approach (DHA) 87
Diversity Triangle, The 49
Drotner, K. and Schrøder, K. 2
Dysthe, Bernhardt and Esbjørn 63
Dysthe, O. 63

echo chamber 23–25
emancipation of the Jews, The 50
Erdi: artefact vignette(s) 106–107; key elements of dialogic experience 107–8
Erdinast–Vulcan, D. 20
ERICArts 26, 29–30
ethical challenges, social media and museums 52
EU 19, 112; and Europeanisation 38
EU policies, virtual spaces and intercultural dialogue 26
European, cultural institution(s) 2
European narratives of belonging: idea of democracy 38–39; shared memory of Holocaust and WWII 38; supranational character 38
European Agenda for Culture 13
European City of Culture initiative 18
European Commission 4, 85; *Citizens' Dialogues* 14; *Digital Cultural Heritage* policy 16; *European Digital Single Market Strategy* 16; intercultural dialogue(s) as means for realising European identity 14; *Social Dialogue* 14; *Structured Dialogue* 14; top–down creation of a common European identity 13
European Cultural Heritage, year of 113
European cultural institutions, as neutral spaces for dialogue 12
European cultural sector, ability to imagine digitally 117
European Digital Single Market Strategy 16
European heritage, darker side of 19
European heritage institutions as neutral, articulation of 12
European people: explained 15–16; responsibility to manage otherness 15
European sense of belonging 38; articulation of 38

European Solidarity Centre (ESC), Gdansk 42
European Union: *see* EU
European values 9; human rights, democracy and the rule of law 9
Europeana 4, 10, 113
Europe in 12 Lessons, European Commission 85
Exhibition, as form of metaphorical dialogue 37
Exhibition design: involving users in 62; *see also* participatory design
exhibitionary complex 67

Facebook 10, 52; enabling impromptu interreligious dialogue, Turku, Finland 21, 30
face–to–face, dialogue(s) as 51
Fake news 26, 102
Farage, N. 88
Faro Convention 9, 10, 13, 19, 109
Faro Convention on the Value of Cultural Heritage for Society: *see Faro Convention*
Farrell–Banks, D. 25, 26
fieldwork: methodology 42–43; museums included 42
filter bubble 23–25
Final Statement of the 10th Council of Europe Conference of Ministers of Culture, "digital revolution," importance of 27
Flickr 10
Floridi, L., expansion of information, as giving individuals more accountability and responsibility to society 38
FOLK: dialogue(s) 65–66; *The Sound of Folk* installation, museum visitors mix, record and edit sounds 64; *see also The Sound of Folk*
FOLK – from racial types to DNA sequences (FOLK): *see FOLK*; *The Sound of Folk*
Folkmann, M. N. 117
Friere, P. 20–21, 63; dialogue as both reflection and action 113
full range of human communication, dialogue(s) as, *vs.* one–to–one encounters 87

Future Workshop *74*
Future Workshop (FW) method: phases of 73; as stabilising factor that allowed pluralisation 76; *see also The Sound of Folk*
Future workshop, the phantasy phase *74*

Galata, Museum of the Sea, Genoa 42–46, *45*, 48, 51
Geographical, boundaries 2
Gere, R. 17
globalisation 1; critiques of 88
Goode, L. 24
Gordon, C. 13, 18
Gove, M. 88
Graham, H.: overcoming glass case as access barrier 67; pluralisation and stability 75
Grorud Youth Council 63, 71; *see also The Sound of Folk*
Guardian, The 86
Guiberneau, M. 98; national identity, elements of 90–91
Gutierrez–Garcia, E., Recalde, M. and Pinera–Camacho, A. 94

Harrison, R. 3, 109
heritage: conceptualisation(s) of 42; "cultural," as set of values and meanings 13; as inherently dialogical 3; as key locus for European identity 18; networked 25; and practices of inclusion and exclusion 13; as prerequisite for EU solidarity 18; as tangible 13
heritage display, digital *vs.* institutional spaces 51
heritage institution(s) 2; re–location in digitial public sphere 28–29; *see also* heritage sites
heritage organisations 27
heritage(s), protecting access to 10
heritage sites: and accommodation of 28–29; Magna Carta Memorial, Runnymede 99
heritage studies 13
historical moment: and ambiguity of, creation of collective memory and sense of historical belonging 91; *vs.* "historical event" 90

Hogsden, C. and Poulter, E. K., digital contact zone 51
Holocaust 2; *see also* The Jewish Museum (JMB), Berlin; National Holocaust Centre and Museum (NHCM) in Laxton UK; the POLIN Museum of the History of Polish Jews in Warsaw
Holt, J. C. 89
Huyssen, A. 90

ICD: *see* intercultural dialogue(s) (ICD)
identities, multiplicity of (interculturality) 54
Illman, R. 21, 30
"imagined communities" 53
immigration: "multicultural others are not seen as constitutive of Europe's own self–understanding" 20; transnational 2
Information Society 10
infrastructure, digital 10
Innocenti, P. 22, 113
institutional space, inherent limitations of, in encouraging conflict 54; and tensions with online spaces for dialogue 39
institution(s): *see* cultural institution(s); heritage institution(s)
institution(s) of memory 38
intellectual property rights 10
Intercult, Torch, C. 1
intercultural 1, 14; dialogue(s): *see* intercultural dialogue(s) (ICD)
intercultural dialogue(s) (ICD) 1, 3; and heritage organisations, compatibility of 27; and negotiating coexistence of commonality and diversity 14; role of 2; spaces for 10; and virtual spaces 26
intercultural exchange and dialogue, utopian approach to potential of heritage and digital technology for 17
interculturalism, defined 13–15
interface, of heritage, dialogue, digital culture 12
interfaces, digital 44
International Council on Monuments and Sites (ICOMOS) 13

interpretation, intentionality of 68–69
intersection(s): of cultures, individuals and experience 40; of heritage, dialogue, digital culture 1, 2; and interstices, of truth 23
interstices: *see* intersection(s)
Iversen, O. S. and Smith, R. C. 40

Jacobi, D. 16
Jewish Museum, The (JMB), Berlin 42, 44, 51, 53–54
Jewish Places, participatory database, The Jewish Museum (JMB), Berlin 53–54
Jones, R. H., Chik, A. and Hafner, C. A. 5
Jungk, R., Future Workshop (FW) method 73

Keller, J., life as dialogic 5
Kent, M. L. 97
KhosraviNik, M. and Unger, J. W. 91, 93
"knowledge infrastructure," as increasing ease of breaking open master narratives 17
Kögler, H. 15, 20

Lähdesmäki, T. 13; cultural and heritage as tools for advancing EU's political project, *vs.* contested domains 14; to heritage(s) 10
Leggewie, C. 2
Levinas, E. 12, 15, 20, 30
"liberation technology" 93
Lindauer, M. 92
listening: civic 39; purposeful 52
Little, K. and Watson, I. 44
Lutz, R., Future Workshop (FW) method 73

Macdonald, S. 90, 99; access to range of previously hidden discourses regarding history and heritage 101; transnational and transcultural European heritage 14
Magna Carta 86; alternate uses of 92; discursive use of by right–wing populists 102; history of 89; meaning communicated in

Index   127

discursive uses of, Twitter 87; "past presencing" of, given relevance in the present through acts of remembering 99; perceived meaning of separate from specific contents 89–90; possible meanings of 92–93; presentation at heritage sites 87
Magna Carta (online), right–wing appropriation of 26
Magna Carta Memorial, Runnymede 99, *100*; display of *Magna Carta* at 92; erected by the American Bar Association *100*
Malraux, R., "museum without walls" 2
Marstine, J. 62
Marwick, A. E. and boyd, d. 92, 93
Mason, R. 14, 92
Mason, R., Whitehead, C. and Graham, H. 43
mass digitisation 27
master narratives, breaking open of through information technology 17
McLean, K. 37
McPhail, M. L. 118
media: changing relation between producers and consumers of 93; *see also* digital media
memory: European, "seven circles of" 2; and history, ambiguity and subjectivity of 90; role of in construction of collective identity 90
Memory and Migration 45
Memory of the World in the Digital Age, The: Digitization and Preservation 11
Message, K. 62
Meyer, M. 62
Mignolo, W. 19
minority groups, promotion of racial hatred against 11
mobilising, dialogue(s) 1–2
Moser, S. 92
Mudec, Museum of Cultures, Milan 42, 44, 45–46
Mueller, N. R., Future Workshop (FW) method 73
multicultural other, mis–recognition of as part of self 20
Murray, J. W. 28

museology: dialogue–driven 39; reflexive, as process of transformation 40
museum displays, as "experimental zones," incorporating ordinary individuals' personal accounts and testimonies 40
Museum for Intercultural Dialogue (MID, Kielcee) 42, 44, 49, 50
Museum of European Cultures, The (MEK), Berlin 42, 44
museum professionals: dialogue as face–to–face activity 22; processes of becoming participants 66
museum(s) 1, 22–23; as broadcaster *vs.* narrowcaster 25; dialogue driven 111; displays 42, 51, 52, 53; and expansion of knowledge perspectives and stabilisation of legitimacy 67; online 25; online moderation 52; positionality of, "Museums are not neutral" 25–26; prioritising of memorial function by 52
museums, bespoke platforms for 52
museum(s) as spaces: dialogic 11, 23; forum and public sphere 37; for social change, dialogue, democracy, human rights and activism 62; of inequality and asymmetrical power 52; at intersection of cultures, individuals and experience 40; as potential "neutral space" for intercultural encounters 25;
Mygind, L., Hällman, A. K. and Bentsen, P. 67

narratives: of belonging 5; idea of democracy 38–39; shared memory of Holocaust and WWII 38; supranational character 38
Näss, H. E. 14
National Museums, The, Liverpool 42
negotiation 22, 25; cultural institutions as spaces for 3
Nelson, H. G. and Stolterman, E. 68–69
net neutrality 27
networked heritage 25
network society, social formation of social and media networks 22

neutrality 25; articulation of European heritage institutions 12; and tensions with positionality 27
New Agenda for Culture, The 119
New Europe, The (app), artefact vignette(s): interactive journey in pop–up living lab 84–85
New European Agenda for Culture, The 10
non–indifference, *vs.* reciprocity 30
Nora, P. 90
normalisation 39–40

online museum: *see* museum(s), online

Page, R., Barton, D., Unger, J. W. and Zappavigna, M. 92
Papacharissi, Z. 115–16
Parry, R. 16
participation, as knowledge process 63
participatory: design 63; challenges to 67; design projects, reflection–in–action, users' or participants' understanding as starting point 69–70; processes, *vs.* "boundary encounter" 62
"participatory museum" 3
participatory process of *The Sound of Folk, The* 72
PD (participatory design): *see* participatory design
pedagogy of feeling 54
Pelinka, A. 87
People's History Museum, The (PHM), Manchester 42
"perceptions of cultural difference," *vs.* constructions of colonialism and racism 19
personal accounts, framing cultural difference as difference in life experience 54
Phipps, A. 19
Pihkala 70
platforms: bespoke 52; digital: and silencing of the other 24; technological limitations built in 26
policy, EU landscape of 9
policy documents 12
POLIN 42, 43, 44, 47, 51; *The Polish Righteous*, POLIN Museum of the History of Polish Jews (Warsaw) 54

politics, right–wing and populist, emergence of 4
polyvocality 26, 39, 41; digitally enhanced 43; of displays 54
populist rhetoric 87–88; "the people" *vs.* "elite" 88; success across Europe 87
positionality, and tensions with neutrality 27
power: asymmetry of 52; dynamics, of digitisation 28; imbalances 93; institutional, museum(s)' 66
power inequality, between audiences and institutions, re–balancing of 39
Proctor, N. 2, 22
Produser, digital media, as both producer and user of 93
Promoting Access to Culture via Digital Means: Policies and Strategies for Audience Development 118
public sphere: digital 12; based on strong civic values 115; heritage institution(s) in 28–29; socially and culturally construction of 16–17

Reckwitz, A. 5
Recommendation concerning the Protection and Promotion of Museums and Collections, their Diversity and their Role in Society 10
Recommendation of the Committee of Ministers to Member States on the Internet of Citizens 27, 28, 29, 109, 119
re–conceptualisation: of dialogue 42; of truth 23
reflection–in–action, Schön, D. 68
reflective, *vs.* reflexive 68
reflective character, of displays 54
"Reflective Devices," artefact vignette 107–8
reflective process 67–68
reflective space 85
reflexive, *vs.* reflective 68
reflexive encounter: dialogue–as–purpose, change as one potential outcome 111; dialogue–as purposive, change as goal 111
reflexivity 68; curatorial 62; as including analysis of contextual relations' influence on design work 68

Report on the Role of Public Arts and Cultural Institutions in the Promotion of Cultural Diversity and Intercultural Dialogue 19
research, empirical 2
responsibility 12
Rheingold, H. 21
Ricœur, P., "historical event" 89–90
right to speak, as contingent on obligation to listen 114; *see also* listening
right–wing populism (RWP) 87; appropriation of narratives of Western superiority in justice and freedom 101
Rigney, A. 39
RWP: *see* right–wing populism (RWP)

Said, E. W. 90
Salisbury Cathedral 100–101; display of *Magna Carta* at 92
Sandell, R. 62
Sanz, N. 23, 24, 29
Sassatelli, M. 18
Schön, D. 85; reflective 67–69
Science, Identity, and Belonging project 111
Second World War 2
self, articulation of 30
sense of belonging 85, 91–92, 99, 101; European 38
Simon, N. 3, 21
Simone, V., dialogic space as "third space" 22
Sky News 88
Smith, L. 13, 20
Smith Pfister, D. and Soliz, J. 3
social media: and changing relation between media producers and consumers of 93; ethical challenges of for museums 52
social media and museums, anti-Semitic comments on 52
social web, revolution of 10
Sound of Folk, The: adjustment of method 75–76; human biological diversity, historical and contemporary research on 64; Norwegian Museum of Science and Technology (NTM) 63; pluralisation and stability 75; power relation level through dialogic collaboration 75; roundtable dialogues 71; use of Future Workshop (FW) method in 79; workshop activities 71; workshops, use of Future Workshop (FW) method in 73–75
Sound of Folk, The, installation: The digital installation *65;* visitors mix sounds expressing diversity of emotions 72
Sound of Folk, The: and museum professionals 62, 64, 66, 67, 70, 73, 76, 79–80; The participatory process of *The Sound of FOLK* lasted over eight workshops 72
Srinivasan, R., Becvar, K. M., Boast, R. and Enote, J. 17
Stewart, J., Zediker, K. and Black, L. 15
subject and other, mutual dependence of 20
subjectivity, articulation of 53
Sunstein, C. 23

Taylor, J. and Gibson, L. K., access as democratisation, critique of 28
Tchen, J. K. W. 3, 15, 39
techno–deterministic approach, to digital heritage, technology/ies 16
techno–literary skills, developing to enable dialogue 118
technology/ies: as actively shaping debates 26; digital 1; and alterity 21; and articulations of fragments 54; capacity to democratise heritage 2; dialogic potential of 3; limited ability to re–configure understandings of alterity 21; potential to break down monologic narratives 41; social and cultural construction of 16–17
tensions, from policy, theory and practice 12
Theunissen, P. and Wan Noordin, W. N. 97
"third space," Bhabba, H. 22
Thornton, M., "civic pluralism," sharing of individuals' stories and memories 21
tools, digital, and articulations of fragments 54
topoi, related to right–wing populist rhetoric 95–96
Torch, C., Intercult 1

130 Index

transcultural, dialogue(s) 2
transcultural dialogue 2
Transformation Machine, The 117; *Deletion Bureau*, altering museum databases to reflect evolving ; notion of "European–ness" 60; as speculative artefact 60; "futurescaping" project 60–61
transnationalism 46
truth, as emergent, relational and intertextual, re–conceptualisation of 23
Tucker, J. A., Guess, A., Barbera, P., Vaccari, C., Sigel, A., Sanovich, S., Stukal, D. and Nyhan, B. 94
Turku, Finland, impromptu interreligious dialogue enabled by Facebook 21
"Turn to openness," cultural 62
Twitter 52; access to range of previously hidden discourses 101, 102–3; apparent dialogic limitations of 94; asynchronous and asymmetrical dialogic encounters, *vs.* symmetric and face–to–face 97; dialogic potential of 96–97; dialogic role of retweet and "reply" function 97; *Magna Carta* on 93; rhetorical use of *Magna Carta* to encourage nationalism 101; as space for potential dialogic encounters 87

UK Government 4
UKIP: *see* United Kingdom Independence Party (UKIP)
UNESCO: digital cultural assets, digitalisation and preservation of 11
UNESCO/UBC's Vancouver Declaration on *The Memory of the World in the Digital Age: Digitization and Preservation* 11
United Kingdom EU referendum (Brexit): *see* Brexit

United Kingdom Independence Party (UKIP) 86

values, flagship European 2
Van den Akker, C. and Legêne, S. 17
Van Dijk, J. 4, 22, 24, 118, 119
Vergo, P. 3
Vidal, R. V. 73
video testimonies, as pivotal to constructing sense of shared history 53
Virtual Shtetl, The, POLIN Museum of the History of Polish Jews (Warsaw) 53
virtual spaces 10
visitor–generated contributions 40–41; *see also* participatory design
visitor participation, as form of co–production, *vs.* glass case exhibitionary complex 67
visualisation, The New Europe (app) 84–85

Wales 86
Warren, W. L. 89, 99
Watt, N. 88
Weber, R., reflective *vs.* reflexive 68
Wharton, E. 20
White Paper on ICD 9, 19, 109, 119; cultural heritage as space for dialogue 14; digital platforms as intrinsically "open" space 18
White Paper on Intercultural Dialogue – Living Together As Equals in Dignity: *see White Paper on ICD*
Witcomb, A, "pedagogy of feeling" 54
Wodak, R. 87, 95, 96
Wodak, R., and KhosraviNik, M. 87
Wong, A. 52
Wood, J. 114, 117

Young, I. M. 25
YouTube 10, 52

For Product Safety Concerns and Information please contact our EU representative GPSR@taylorandfrancis.com
Taylor & Francis Verlag GmbH, Kaufingerstraße 24, 80331 München, Germany